ADVOCACY JOURNALISTS

A Biographical Dictionary of Writers and Editors

Edd Applegate

THE SCARECROW PRESS, INC.
Lanham, Maryland • Toronto • Plymouth, UK
2009

SCARECROW PRESS, INC.

Published in the United States of America
by Scarecrow Press, Inc.
A wholly owned subsidary of
The Rowman & Littlefield Publishing Group, Inc.
4501 Forbes Boulevard, Suite 200, Lanham, Maryland 20706
www.scarecrowpress.com

Estover Road
Plymouth PL6 7PY
United Kingdom

British Library Cataloguing in Publication Information Available

Library of Congress Cataloging-in-Publication Data

Applegate, Edd.
  Advocacy journalists : a biographical dictionary of writers and editors / Edd
Applegate.
     p. cm.
  Includes bibliographical references and index.
  ISBN 978-0-8108-6928-8 (hardcover : alk. paper) — ISBN 978-0-8108-6929-5
(ebook)
  1. Journalists—United States—Biography—Dictionaries. 2. Journalism—
United States—History—Bio-bibliography. I. Title.
  PN4871.A52 2009
  070.92′273—dc22
  [B]   2009001545

∞ ™ The paper used in this publication meets the minimum requirements of
American National Standard for Information Sciences—Permanence of Paper
for Printed Library Materials, ANSI/NISO Z39.48-1992.
Manufactured in the United States of America.

For Eva, the love of my life.

Contents

Acknowledgments

I WISH TO THANK MR. STEPHEN RYAN, my editor, for believing that this book would be a worthy addition to Scarecrow's list. I also wish to thank the other editors and staff at Scarecrow for making this book possible.

I wish to thank the various librarians at the James E. Walker Library, Middle Tennessee State University, Murfreesboro, for their assistance.

Introduction

ADVOCACY JOURNALISM HAS BEEN practiced for several hundred years. Indeed, advocacy journalism is in all likelihood the oldest form of journalism. It appears frequently whenever journalists desire to advocate their beliefs or ideas about major political or social problems. However, repercussions sometimes occur when journalists feel the need to advocate their beliefs. In 1584, in England, William Carter was hanged for printing pamphlets that defied the Tudors. Nathaniel Butter and Thomas Archer were censored in the early 1620s when they published corantos criticizing James I's foreign policy. Nicholas Bourne, Nathaniel Butter, and Thomas Archer, after his release from prison, started other corantos that were eventually restricted in 1632. Such actions by those in authority caused John Milton to argue for a free press in his *Areopagitica*, which was published in 1644. William Walwyn, Henry Robinson, Richard Overton, and John Lilburne argued for a free press as well.

In the new world, during the colonial period and the 1800s, journalists employed advocacy journalism to present their perspectives about political and social issues, including war; journalists of the 1900s, particularly those writing after World War I and World War II, employed advocacy journalism as well. During the so-called new journalism years, especially during the 1960s and 1970s, journalists employed advocacy journalism to present their perspectives about Vietnam, drugs, and the rights of minorities and women, among other issues.

WHAT IS ADVOCACY JOURNALISM?

Ernest C. Hynds defined advocacy journalism in these terms: "Advocacy journalism is based on the premise that the journalist has both a right and an obligation to become involved in the events that he reports. The advocate . . . says that since objectivity in reporting cannot be obtained, it should not be attempted. The reporter should instead tell the truth of the event or situation as he sees it."[1]

In essence, the writer presents his or her position when discussing a specific topic. John L. Hulteng wrote, "We need exposure to the opinions of others—and not just the opinions of those with an ax to grind, the political leaders, the special-interest spokesmen. We need the aid we can get from the analysis and interpretation provided by persons who are steeped in the flow of events but who can keep those events in reasonably dispassionate perspective."[2]

In short, in order for citizens to learn about what is happening in society and politics, they must be willing to read or listen to various views or interpretations by those who work in the media, particularly those who work for the major newspapers and magazines.

THE PURPOSE OF THIS BOOK

The primary purpose of this biographical dictionary is to present information about writers who practiced advocacy journalism and editors who encouraged such writing in the pages of their publications. Coverage is heaviest of writers and editors working in the United States during the last one hundred years or so, but important writers are included from earlier centuries and other countries as well. Most, if not all, of these writers and editors have been identified by more than one source as having written advocacy journalism or accepted such writing. A few of these writers, such as

Carleton Beals, George Creel, and Matthew Josephson, practiced muckraking journalism, too.

Each biographical sketch begins with the writer's name and dates of birth and death, if found. Then the writer's life is summarized chronologically, with information pertaining to his or her professional career and major works. In some cases, comments by others about the writer's work have been included. Readers interested in learning more about a writer or editor should begin with that person's works listed at the end of each entry. Of course, the selected bibliography at the end of the book will also help.

NOTES

1. Ernest C. Hynds, *American Newspapers in the 1980s* (New York: Hastings House, 1980), 173–174.

2. John L. Hulteng, *The Opinion Function: Editorial and Interpretive Writing for the News Media* (New York: Harper & Row, 1973), 3.

Lyman Abbott
(1835-1922)

LYMAN ABBOTT, JOURNALIST AND CLERGYMAN, was born on December 18, 1835, in Roxbury, Massachusetts, to Harriet Vaughan Abbott and Jacob Abbott. Although he moved with his family to Farmington, Maine, his mother died several years later, when he was seven. His father moved to New York City primarily to manage a school, but Abbott remained in Farmington, where he was raised and educated by relatives.

When Abbott was in his teens, his father encouraged him to open a business or continue his education. Abbott enrolled at New York University, from which he received his bachelor's degree in 1853. After learning about law, he accepted a position at a firm that had been founded by his older brothers, Austin and Vaughn.

Abbott was admitted to the bar in 1856. A year later he married Abby Francis Hamlin, a distant relative. Although law undoubtedly was interesting, Abbott was influenced by his childhood desires and Henry Ward Beecher's "great revival" of 1858 to become a minister. Abbott was ordained in 1860 and became the pastor of the Congregational Church in Terre Haute, Indiana, later the same year. Abbott attended to his parishioners who had mixed feelings about the war. Indeed, some favored the South, while some favored the North.

In 1865, Abbott returned to New York, where he became executive secretary of the American Union Commission, an organization formed by various denominations for the purpose of helping the government in its efforts to reconstruct the South. A year later, in addition to his duties with the American Union Commission, he became pastor of the New England Congregational Church in New York City. Eventually Abbott became general secretary of the American Freedmen's Union Commission, which had grown out of the American Union Commission, and edited the organization's monthly publication, *American Freedman*.

Abbott's wife contracted tuberculosis. In 1869, Abbott resigned from the American Freedmen's Union Commission and the church and moved with his family to Cornwall, New York, where he tended to his wife's needs and worked as a freelance writer. He contributed book reviews to *Harper's Monthly Magazine* and wrote two books on Bible study: *Jesus of Nazareth: His Life and Teachings* and *Old Testament Shadows of New Testament Truths*, which were published in 1869 and 1870, respectively.

Within two years Abbott became editor of *The Illustrated Christian Weekly*, a new publication published by the American Tract Society of New York. Abbott contributed the column "Outlook," in which he discussed political and social issues, among other topics.

Primarily because of his success as an editor as well as his relationship with Henry Ward Beecher, Abbott was offered the position of associate editor of the *Christian Union* in August 1876. The publication, which resembled a weekly newspaper, had been edited by Beecher since 1870. However, when Beecher was charged with committing adultery in 1875, the publication's popularity declined. When Abbott started work in September 1876, the circulation was approximately fifteen thousand. He was determined to increase the publication's circulation by changing readers' opinions of it.

Although Beecher was active in the publication, he retired in 1881; Abbott became the editor-in-chief. Under Abbott's guidance, the publication became a success. Abbott employed his wife and other family members to fill certain positions. For instance, when Lawson Valentine, a friend who had served as president of the company that published the weekly, died in 1891, Abbott's son, Lawrence, became the president.

Abbott changed the focus of the publication, too. In addition to publishing articles about religion, he published articles that concerned societal and political issues. Indeed, topics such as conservation, immigration, rights of minorities, and temperance were discussed. Later, the periodical's pages included articles about the welfare of the poor working classes. Abbott advocated for shorter working hours and better working conditions, among other issues. However, he was opposed to the questionable methods labor unions occasionally employed on behalf of their members. Abbott published several articles that discussed poverty.

Abbott became active in several organizations such as the American Economic Association and the Indian Rights Association. For the former, he published a series on socialism. For the latter, he published articles about Native American issues. He advocated that land that had been taken from Native Americans be returned to them. He also advocated that education be provided to the various tribes. Abbott believed that whites had an obligation to help Native Americans acclimate to society. Without question, he influenced the writing of the Dawes Act, which was passed in 1887.

After Beecher died in 1887, Abbott was offered Beecher's position of pastor at the Plymouth Congregational Church in Brooklyn. Primarily because he would not give up his duties at the publication, an associate pastor was hired to help him. Abbott divided his time between the church and the publication.

Abbott changed the *Christian Union*'s format from a newspaper to a magazine in 1891. Two years later he changed the publication's name to *The Outlook* primarily to reflect the magazine's content, which had become more topical and less religious. Eventually, perhaps as a result of such changes, the magazine's circulation increased to more than one hundred thousand, which attracted more advertisers.

Abbott advocated incorporating evolutionary theory into theology in his book *The Evolution of Christianity*, which was published in 1892 and which was, to say the least, controversial. Abbott claimed that knowledge was good for humanity as long as it advanced the Kingdom of God. He believed strongly in Christianity, advocating that it was above other religions.

Although he had continued to divide his time between the magazine and the Plymouth Congregational Church, Abbott's health deteriorated. Consequently, he left the church in 1898. However, he remained at *The Outlook*.

President Theodore Roosevelt, an avid reader of Abbott's publication and books, summoned him to the White House in 1901. As a result of his meeting with the president, Abbott realized that he and Roosevelt thought alike on many issues. Subsequently, Abbott's publication became somewhat of a voice for Roosevelt's progressive policies, something that Abbott would not necessarily have done for other politicians or their administrations.

Although he had edited several books about Henry Ward Beecher, Abbott's biography of his friend, *Henry Ward Beecher*, was published in 1903.

Abbott's wife died suddenly in 1907 while they were vacationing in Germany. To take his mind off of his wife's death and to ease his suffering, Abbott devoted his time to the magazine and to writing books.

Primarily because of their friendship, Abbott encouraged Roosevelt to serve as an editor of *The Outlook* after he left office. Roosevelt became an editor in 1909. When Roosevelt ran for the presidency in 1912, Abbott, reluctantly, supported him in the pages of the magazine, which caused readers who opposed Roosevelt to cancel their subscriptions.

Roosevelt resigned from the magazine in 1914, but the publication's editorial policy failed to change as a result. In fact, like Roosevelt, the magazine favored military action after the Germans sank the *Lusitania* in 1915. Abbott, along with other well-known men, signed a petition addressed to President Woodrow Wilson opposing peace negotiations with Germany. He approved of the Espionage Act (1917) and the Sedition Act (1918), which limited freedom of expression by those who opposed the war.

In 1918, Abbott reduced the number of hours he worked at the magazine primarily because of his age and ill health. He died in New York City in 1922.

The Outlook was never the same after his death. In fact, his heirs sold the magazine in 1927. Although it eventually died, it was resurrected with a new title. However, the publication ceased to exist in 1935.

SELECTED WORKS

Articles

"The Wages System," *Forum* (July 1890)
"Industrial Democracy," *Forum* (August 1890)
"Compulsory Arbitration," *Arena* (December 1892)
"Religious Teaching in Our Public Schools," *Century* (April 1895)
"Our Indian Problem," *North American Review* (December 1898)
"The Advance of Women," *World's Work* (July 1904)
"What Money Is Really Good For," *Ladies' Home Journal* (September 1908)
"Why the Vote Would Be Injurious to Women," *Ladies' Home Journal* (February 1910)

Books

The Rights of Man: A Study in Twentieth Century Problems (1901)
Why Women Do Not Wish the Suffrage (1904)
The Industrial Problem: Being the William Levi Bull Lectures for the Year 1905 (1905)
Reminiscences (1915)
What Christianity Means to Me: A Spiritual Autobiography (1921)

REFERENCES

Abbott, Lyman. *Reminiscences*. Boston: Houghton Mifflin, 1915.
———. *What Christianity Means to Me*. New York: Macmillan, 1921.
Brown, Ira V. *Lyman Abbott, Christian Evolutionist: A Study in Religious Liberalism*. Cambridge, Mass.: Harvard University Press, 1953.
"Dr. Lyman Abbott Dies in 87th Year." *New York Times*, October 23, 1922, 1.

Lippy, Charles H., ed. *Religious Periodicals of the United States: Academic and Scholarly Journals.* Westport, Conn.: Greenwood, 1986.
Wagenknecht, Edward. *American Profile 1900–1909.* Amherst: University of Massachusetts Press, 1982.

Joseph Addison
(1672–1719)

JOSEPH ADDISON, WHO WAS BORN IN 1672, had written poetry and literary criticism and had traveled to France and Italy before he had composed one article for Richard Steele's *The Tatler*. Unlike Steele, Addison came from a refined family, and his social class awareness helped him immensely. When he dedicated a poem to Lord Chancellor Somers, Somers reciprocated. For instance, on learning that Addison wished to travel and write, Somers helped him obtain a yearly pension of three hundred pounds from the Crown. Thus encouraged, Addison left England for the Continent and upon his return wrote *Travels*, which he dedicated to Somers. In 1704, he wrote the heroic poem "The Campaign," which celebrated the battle of Blenheim. The poem was read by the Lord-Treasurer Godolphin, who not only approved of it but bestowed on Addison the vacant position of commissioner of appeals.

In 1706, Addison was appointed undersecretary of state, and he was elected to Parliament in 1708. During these years, he wrote operas, comedies, and poetry. He moved to Ireland in 1709, when he became secretary to the Marquess of Wharton, who had been appointed Lord-Lieutenant of Ireland. Although he contributed to Steele's *The Tatler*, readers did not recognize his distinct style of writing until *The Spectator* appeared on March 1, 1711.[1]

The Spectator and *The Tatler* were similar in appearance. However, according to G. Gregory Smith, "the *Tatler* stands first in importance, not merely because it came as a kind of prelude to the *Spectator*, but because it was the direct model for the literary plan and details of the later journal."[2]

Thus, it could be said that *The Tatler* was *The Spectator* in the rough or that *The Spectator* was the polished *Tatler*. The same could be said about Steele and Addison. As Austin Dobson wrote, "There is little doubt that in the finely-wrought La Bruyere–like sketches of Tom Folio, Ned Softly, and the Political Upholsterer, in the Rabelaisian 'Frozen Voices' and the delightful 'Adventures of a Shilling,' Addison attained a level higher than anything at which his friend had aimed."[3]

The Spectator reflected Addison's philosophy. According to Edward and Lillian Bloom:

> A disciple of Sir Andrew and his mercantile code, Addison is also respectful of Sir Roger and the "landed" principle. He is a traditionalist who stands on the side of change when the new contributes to national order and prosperity and to learning and civility. He is a Whig who moves with ease among moderate Tories. He praises the beauty of faith, but his is a belief derived more often than not from earth-bound demonstrations. Arguing for tolerance as a token of good nature, he is a staunch Anglican who extends the hand of Christian fellowship to orthodox dissenters and turns his back on Catholics.[4]

This philosophy was voiced by personae in at least 274 of the 555 issues. Steele's philosophy was voiced by other characters in 236 issues. Eustace Budgell, a clergyman, was responsible for 28 issues, and other contributors were responsible for the remaining 17 issues. Considering the various characters, such as Sir Roger de Coverley (the most famous), a Templar, Will Honeycomb, a Clergyman, Captain Sentry, and Sir Andrew Freeport, Addison undoubtedly was responsible for the first three.

The Spectator, which appeared daily until December 6, 1712, was filled with entertaining as well as informative pieces, including essays, stories, and articles of criticism. It was read by the poor as well as the rich, and unlike *The Tatler*, which was read mostly by men in coffeehouses, *The Spectator* was read by women as well as men, in homes and coffeehouses. Together, the two publications molded ideas and developed tastes, and helped establish the magazine as a journalistic as well as a literary product.

Joseph Addison saw numerous imitators of *The Tatler* and *The Spectator* before his death in 1719.

SELECTED WORK

The Spectator (1711–1712)

NOTES

1. G. Gregory Smith, ed., *The Spectator, with Introduction by Austin Dobson* (New York: Scribner's, 1897), xx.
2. Smith, ed., *The Spectator*, xii.
3. Smith, ed., *The Spectator*, xxi.
4. Edward A. Bloom and Lillian D. Bloom, *Joseph Addison's Sociable Animal: In the Marketplace, on the Hustings, in the Pulpit* (Providence, R.I.: Brown University Press, 1971), 7–8.

REFERENCES

Bloom, Edward A., and Lillian D. Bloom. *Joseph Addison's Sociable Animal: In the Marketplace, on the Hustings, in the Pulpit.* Providence, R.I.: Brown University Press, 1971.
Otten, Robert M. *Joseph Addison.* Boston: Twayne, 1982.
Smith, G. Gregory, ed. *The Spectator, with Introduction by Austin Dobson.* New York: Scribner's, 1897.
Smithers, Peter. *The Life of Joseph Addison.* Oxford: Clarendon, 1954.

Joseph Alsop
(1910–1989)

JOURNALIST AND COLUMNIST JOSEPH ALSOP was born on October 11, 1910, to Corinne and Joseph Alsop, in Avon, Connecticut. His parents, who were active in Connecticut politics, lived on a farm. Alsop spent several years learning about agriculture before his parents sent him to the Groton School in Massachusetts. In 1928, he enrolled at Harvard University, where he enjoyed learning the liberal arts.

Upon graduation in 1932, Alsop became a reporter for the *New York Herald Tribune*, for which he wrote in-depth articles about the Hauptmann trial. Alsop received considerable praise for his comprehensive stories. The editorial staff sent Alsop to Washington, D.C., to cover politics several years later. Within a year, he met Robert Kintner, another *Herald Tribune* staff member, and they began the nationally syndicated political column "The Capitol Parade."

For three years the column clarified political issues. In collaboration with Turner Catledge, Alsop wrote *The 168 Days*, which was published in 1938. This book discussed the crisis that surrounded the United States Supreme Court after President Franklin Roosevelt decided that the Court should be enlarged. In collaboration with Kintner, Alsop wrote *Men around the President* in 1939 and *American White Paper: The Story of American Diplomacy and the Second World War* in 1940. These books concerned Roosevelt's administrative advisers and personal confidants and the president's foreign policy before World War II.

Alsop's partnership with Kintner ended in 1940 when he enlisted in the U.S. Navy. He resigned a year later and joined the U.S. Army, specifically General Claire Chennault's staff in China. Alsop was sent to Manila in 1941 and was captured and imprisoned by the Japanese for a year. When he was released, he returned to the United States, where he became a civilian official in the Lend-Lease Mission to Chunking. Subsequently, he returned to China, and General Chennault had him commissioned as an officer in the army air force. Alsop returned to the United States after the war and, together with his younger brother, Stewart, started the column "Matter of Fact" in 1946.

Syndicated through the *New York Herald Tribune*, the column concerned more than just politics in Washington. Indeed, not only did it contain information about the political scene, but its writers often attacked or defended certain political actions or figures. Occasionally they would predict certain political or military actions. The Alsops denounced Soviet expansionism while they advocated a strong national defense. They condemned Senator Joseph McCarthy, who falsely accused certain citizens of being Communists or Communist sympathizers.

In 1954, the Alsops collaborated on the book *We Accuse! The Story of the Miscarriage of American Justice in the Case of J. Robert Oppenheimer*, in which they defended physicist J. Robert Oppenheimer, who had been charged by certain individuals to be a risk to national security.

The column contained both bylines until Stewart accepted an editorial position with the *Saturday Evening Post* in 1958, the year their second book, *The Reporter's Trade*, was published.

Alsop continued the column alone. When the *Herald Tribune* ceased publication, the column was syndicated through the *Los Angeles Times* Syndicate. Alsop, a defender of the Cold War and later the Vietnam War, married Susan Patten in 1961. This marriage, which did not produce any children, ended in divorce in the 1970s.

Joseph Alsop retired the column in 1974, the year his brother died of leukemia. Alsop had grown tired of writing the column; he also had other interests, including archeology and art. Indeed, his book *From the Silent Earth: A Report on the Greek Bronze Age*, which had been published in 1964, had been praised for its keen insight into a period of ancient history about which little had been written. In 1982, after having conducted several years of research, he wrote *The Rare Art Traditions: The History of Art Collecting and Its Linked Phenomena Wherever These Have Appeared*, which explored the world of art and art collecting from a historical perspective. The same year his book *FDR: A Centenary Remembrance*, which was a text filled with more than two hundred lavish photographs, was published. The book was praised for Alsop's revelations, which tended to make Roosevelt less enigmatic than other biographies.

Alsop died in August 1989.

SELECTED WORKS

"The Capitol Parade" (column with Robert Kintner, 1937–1940)
"Matter of Fact" (column with Stewart Alsop, 1946–1958)
"Matter of Fact" (column, 1958–1974)

REFERENCES

Almquist, Leann Grabavoy. *Joseph Alsop and American Foreign Policy: Journalist as Advocate*. Lanham, Md.: University Press of America, 1993.
Alsop, Joseph, with Adam Platt. *I've Seen the Best of It: Memoirs*. New York: Norton, 1992.
Yoder, Edwin. *Joe Alsop's Cold War: A Study of Journalistic Influence and Intrigue*. Chapel Hill: University of North Carolina Press, 1995.

Stewart Alsop
(1914–1974)

BORN ON MAY 17, 1914, in Avon, Connecticut, to Corinne and Joseph Alsop, Stewart Alsop learned about agriculture on his parents' farm before he attended the Groton School in Massachusetts.

Upon his graduation from the prestigious preparatory school, Steward Alsop entered Yale University, from which he received a bachelor's degree in 1936. Alsop was hired as an editor by Doubleday Doran and Company, publishers, and wrote articles for several magazines.

When the United States entered World War II, Alsop tried to enlist in the U.S. Army but was rejected for medical reasons. He persevered, however, and in 1942 joined the King's Royal Rifle Corps of England. Alsop was commissioned an officer and had been promoted to the rank of captain when he was transferred in 1944 to the U.S. Army's Office of Strategic Services. The same year he married Patricia Hankey, who was from England. Alsop parachuted into France and, on assignment, joined the French underground. When the war ended in Europe, he was awarded the Croix de Guerre with Palm. Alsop then returned to the United States.

In collaboration with Thomas Braden, Stewart Alsop wrote *Sub Rosa: The O.S.S. and American Espionage*, which was published in 1946 and depicted realistically the intelligence unit's activities in certain campaigns of the war.

With his older brother Joseph, Alsop started the political column "Matter of Fact," which was syndicated through the *New York Herald Tribune*. By 1950, the column was published in more than 125 newspapers. The Alsops discussed not only national and international politics but provided various predictions, some of which came true. Occasionally filled with gossip, the column also advocated certain positions, especially when the Alsops' convictions about those positions were strong. Usually one brother stayed in Washington, D.C., primarily to conduct interviews with politicians and other officials, while the other brother traveled abroad to gather material. As a result, their column presented subjects that were current and topical, and they enjoyed a certain amount of credibility. The Alsops disagreed on certain topics, however, and these disagreements tended to strain their collaborating efforts. Before they separated in 1958, they had collaborated on the books *We Accuse! The Story of the Miscarriage of American Justice in the Case of J. Robert Oppenheimer* and *The Reporter's Trade*, which were published in 1954 and 1958, respectively.

Alsop became the political editor of the *Saturday Evening Post*. This position lasted until the magazine ceased publication ten years later in 1968. His book *The Center: People and Power in Political Washington* was published the same year and explored several federal institutions, including the Central Intelligence Agency, the State Department, and the Pentagon. Alsop acknowledged that Washington contained "many Washingtons" but that his book concerned the Washington that political journalists like himself found intriguing. After leaving the *Saturday Evening Post*, he wrote a political column for *Newsweek*.

Stewart Alsop had an unusual form of leukemia. His brother Joseph provided him with numerous blood transfusions, which seemed to force the disease into remission. He wrote the memoir *Stay of Execution: A Sort of Memoir*, in which he explored his life and the disease that eventually killed him. The book was published in 1973, and Alsop died on May 26, 1974. Alsop and his wife had six children.

SELECTED WORKS

"Matter of Fact" (column with Joseph Alsop, 1945–1958)
The Reporter's Trade (with Joseph Alsop, 1958)
The Center: People and Power in Political Washington (1968)

REFERENCES

Alsop, Stewart. *Stay of Execution: A Sort of Memoir.* Philadelphia: Lippincott, 1973.
Merry, Robert W. *Taking on the World: Joseph and Stewart Alsop—Guardians of the American Century.* New York: Viking, 1996.

Michael J. Arlen (1930–)

Michael J. Arlen was born in London, England, on December 9, 1930, but moved to the United States with his parents, Michael and Atalanta Arlen, when he was ten. He attended Harvard University from 1948 to 1952 and then worked as a reporter for *Life* magazine for four years. In 1966, he became a staff writer and television critic for *The New Yorker*, for which he wrote numerous reviews and articles. His criticism, which was not so much about television as it was about American culture or American society, discussed the weaknesses and possible effects of certain programs, including the evening news. His first book, *Living Room War*, which was a collection of critical articles, was published in 1969. In the book's introduction, Arlen explained the title:

> I call this book *Living Room War* not because I especially like the piece I first attached the title to . . . but because quite a number of the pieces are about the war and television—because during the period I was writing them the war seemed to be the central fact in American life, seemed to be there, whether one talked about it or not at first, whether one claimed to be bored by it or not, later offended, later outraged, later bored. It was a changing shape beneath everything else in American life in that period, in a way that no other war we'd experienced had been, and most of us knew about it, felt about it, from television.[1]

A year later, *Exiles*, a memoir of Arlen's search for his father, was published. The book was a minor effort.

In 1973, Arlen turned his attention to the Hanrahan trial in *An American Verdict*. Using short, direct sentences, Arlen told of the questionable shootings of two Black Panther party members by Chicago police officers and the subsequent trial of State's Attorney Edward Hanrahan of Cook County and the police officers involved in the shootings. According to Benjamin De Mott, Arlen's method of writing was impressionistic: "Scenes and snippets of testimony from the trial are interspersed with short takes on the character of Mayor Daley, the birth and history of the Panthers, developments in the culture of street gangs, a copy awards night, the Chicago Irish in fact and fiction, Campaign '72, and a number of other subjects."[2] Arlen attempted to connect the pieces even if some did not fit, much as he had in his collection of articles. The latter, however, contained a logical progression and consequently was better received by the critics.

In *Passage to Ararat*, which was published in 1975, Arlen searched his father's homeland, Armenia, and told of his heritage, including the brutality of Turkey toward the Armenian women and children at the turn of the century. The book exhibited, perhaps better than any other, Arlen's power of writing and earned the National Book Award in contemporary affairs in 1976.

Other collections of articles appeared. For instance, *The View from Highway 1: Essays on Television* was published in 1976 and concerned different topics in television news and entertainment. *Thirty Seconds*, which was published in 1980, examined the six-month effort by advertising agency personnel to produce a thirty-second television commercial for AT&T. Arlen not only observed the process of creating and producing a commercial but also interviewed those involved. The book presented a candid look at another aspect of television. *The Camera Age: Essays on Television* contained twenty-five reviews and articles. At least thirteen concerned news or other "fact" broadcasting, while eight discussed dramatic series or films. The book, which was published in 1981, was praised by critics who appreciated the author's literary style as well as insight.

Arlen's unique style of writing was not limited to criticism for *The New Yorker*, however. His enlightening articles were published in the *Atlantic Monthly*, *Cosmopolitan*, *Esquire*, *Harper's*, *Holiday*, the *New York Times Magazine*, *Saturday Review*, and other publications.

Say Goodbye to Sam, Arlen's first novel, was published in 1984 to mixed reviews.

Arlen's articles and collections were examples of advocacy journalism primarily because they criticized the various kinds of programs that were broadcast on a popular medium. More important, the same articles and collections criticized American society for allowing such a medium to dominate American lives.

Several of his collections were published with new introductions in the 1990s and early 2000s.

SELECTED WORKS

Living Room War (1969)
An American Verdict (1973)
The View from Highway 1: Essays on Television (1976)
Thirty Seconds (1980)
The Camera Age: Essays on Television (1981)

NOTES

1. Michael J. Arlen, *Living Room War* (New York: Viking, 1969), xi.
2. Benjamin De Mott, "Alone in Cover-Up Country," *Atlantic* (October 1973): 117–118.

REFERENCES

Arlen, Michael J. *Living Room War*. New York: Viking, 1969.
———. *An American Verdict*. New York: Doubleday, 1973.
———. *The View from Highway 1: Essays on Television*. New York: Farrar, Straus & Giroux, 1976.

———. *Thirty Seconds*. New York: Farrar, Straus & Giroux, 1980.

———. *The Camera Age: Essays on Television*. New York: Farrar, Straus & Giroux, 1981.

Brustein, Robert. "For Those Who Have No Interest in Television." *New York Times Book Review* 86 (April 12, 1981): 3.

De Mott, Benjamin. "A Word from the Sponsors." *New York Times Book Review* 85 (May 4, 1980): 12.

McConnell, Robert. "The Television Criticism of Michael Arlen, 1966–1981: A Study of Arlen's Aesthetic Standards." Ph.D. diss., Ohio University, Athens, 1983.

———. "Interview with Michael Arlen." *Literature Film Quarterly* 16, no. 2 (1988): 119.

Spear, Marilyn W. "Michael Arlen's Journal Records Armenia's Pain." *Telegram & Gazette* (Worchester, Mass.) (April 15, 1989), 23.

James Baldwin
(1924–1987)

BORN IN HARLEM ON AUGUST 2, 1924, James Baldwin became one of the foremost essayists and novelists of the 1960s. Throughout his writing he explored and deplored the injustices committed against African Americans. His essays, which moved critics and politicians, appealed to the human conscience to look beneath the skin and to think in terms of equality.

Baldwin, whose stepfather was a minister from New Orleans, preached "hell fire and damnation" at Harlem's Fireside Pentecostal Church before he was fifteen. After three years, however, he resigned because of a growing interest in writing.

When he graduated from De Witt Clinton High School in 1942, Baldwin worked briefly in Belle Meade, New Jersey. Because the country was at war, employment was available to those who wanted jobs. He then moved from Belle Meade to Greenwich Village, where he worked during the day and wrote at night. He reviewed books about the black problem for such publications as the *Nation*, *New Leader*, and *Commentary*. He also wrote two books that helped him earn two fellowships, but the books were not published.

Finally, after five years of frustration, he moved to France. Although his life in Paris was free in the sense that he experienced little or no discrimination, he often suffered from not earning enough to live. Nonetheless, he remained in France for ten years.

Baldwin's first, partly autobiographical novel, *Go Tell It on the Mountain*, which concerned a confused Harlem youth named John Grimes and his religious family, was published in 1953. The book was critically acclaimed for its insight into the American racial problem. His next book, *Notes of a Native Son*, which appeared in 1955, was a collection of essays that had appeared in several magazines, including *Commentary* and *Partisan Review*. The essays vividly penetrated the social injustices and prejudices of American society. Immediately, Baldwin was recognized as a humanitarian spokesperson for the oppressed. *Notes* was followed by another novel entitled *Giovanni's Room*, which explored homosexuality.

While Baldwin continued to write novels, he contributed essays to such periodicals as *Harper's*, *The Reporter*, *The New Yorker*, *Nation*, *Esquire*, *Commentary*, and *Partisan Review*.

In 1961, *Another Country* was published. A novel, it concerned an African American woman and a white man who discarded the rules imposed on them by a basically white society and subsequently lived for themselves. Baldwin's second collection of essays, *Nobody Knows My Name: More Notes of a Native Son*, was published the same year. In 1963, in *The Fire Next Time*, Baldwin returned to the problems caused by racial prejudice with power and magnitude. In two essays, both of which were in the form of letters, Baldwin recounted his experience as a preacher in Harlem and examined the movement founded by the Black Muslims. Any white who read the book sensed the degradation that confronted most African Americans.

In addition to writing such novels as *Tell Me How Long the Train's Been Gone* (1968), *If Beale Street Could Talk* (1974), and *Just above My Head* (1979) and such collections of essays as *No Name in the Streets* (1972) and *The Devil Finds Work* (1976), Baldwin also explored the black problem in the plays *The Amen Corner* and *Blues for Mister Charlie*. Although the plays were produced and Baldwin's messages were clear, neither play had the impact of his essays.

Baldwin died of cancer in 1987.

SELECTED WORKS

Go Tell It on the Mountain (1953)
Notes of a Native Son (1955)
Nobody Knows My Name: More Notes of a Native Son (1961)
The Fire Next Time (1963)
No Name in the Streets (1972)
The Devil Finds Work (1976)

REFERENCES

Gottfried, Ted. *James Baldwin: Voice from Harlem*. New York: Watts, 1997.

Leeming, David. *James Baldwin: A Biography*. New York: Knopf, 1994.

Pratt, Louis H. *James Baldwin*. Boston: Twayne, 1978.

Weatherby, W. J. *James Baldwin: Artist on Fire: A Portrait*. New York: Fine, 1989.

Carleton Beals
(1893–1979)

CARLETON BEALS, THE GRANDSON OF Carrie Nation, was born in 1893, in Medicine Lodge, Kansas. His father, Leon Beals, was a lawyer and journalist. When Beals was three, his family moved to California, where he attended public schools in Pasadena.

Beals graduated from high school in 1911 and worked at a number of jobs, including foundryman, waiter, grocery clerk, cashier, cowboy, shoe salesman, and tutor, while attending the University of California. Beals won the Bonnheim Essay Prize twice and the Bryce History Essay Prize once. As a result of his outstanding academic achievement, he was awarded a graduate scholarship to Columbia University.

Although he had studied engineering and mining at the undergraduate level, Beals's interests changed at the graduate level. For instance, he wrote a thesis on the self-sufficient state (economics), earned a Teachers College certificate, and wrote a book on economics that unfortunately was destroyed in a fire. He earned his master of arts degree in 1917.

Writing was now a part of his life. He tried writing short stories but could not find a publisher. Finally, he found a job with the Standard Oil Company of California. However, punching an adding machine in the export department was boring to him. Beals left the company to see the world. Driving a secondhand Ford, he set out for Mexico. Before he reached Mexico City, his car stalled; he rode on rented burros; he walked; and he endured considerable hard-ship—from nearly starving to almost being ambushed by soldiers.

Although he had some money, he was in desperate need of work. Within a few months, he founded the English Preparatory Institute. In addition, he got a job as a teacher, then principal, at the American High School and landed another job as an instructor of English to staff members of President Carranza. These jobs took up most of his time; however, he continued to write. By 1920, when a revolution forced President Carranza to flee, ultimately causing Beals to lose two of his three jobs, he had contributed at least four articles to magazines and had completed a book about Mexico.

Beals left for Spain, where he studied at the University of Madrid, traveled, and wrote articles. About a year later, he moved to Italy, where he studied at the University of Rome, watched Mussolini rise to power, and wrote articles and a book about fascism.

He returned to Mexico City, then New York City. He worked on the books about Mexico and fascism, and both were published in 1923. While living in New York City, he wrote *Brimstone and Chili: A Book of Personal Experiences in the Southwest and in Mexico*. The book was published in 1927, the year General Augusto Sandino led a revolt against the United States Marines who were occupying Nicaragua; the revolt lasted until 1933, when the United States withdrew its forces.

Beals was sent to Nicaragua by the *Nation* to write a series of articles. As Joan Cook wrote, "Mr. Beals . . . made his way from Honduras, partly on horseback, partly on foot, hacking his way through the jungle, accompanied by an escort of Sandinistas."[1] Beals finally reached the general and interviewed him before the marines started their daily bombing mission. His dispatches were published in the *Nation* as well as in newspapers throughout the United States, Europe, and Asia.

Beals returned to the United States in 1929, then headed back to Europe. He revisited Spain and became a close friend of Manual Azana. He traveled to North Africa, Spanish and French Morocco, Algiers, and Tunisia. He journeyed on horseback through the Rif country. He studied Italy under Mussolini, then visited Greece and Turkey. Later he traveled into the Soviet Union and part of Germany. Beals continued to contribute articles based on his travels and observations to the *Nation* and the *New Republic*, among other publications.

He returned to New York City, then set off on a journey through the Oaxaca Mountains. The book based on this journey, *Mexican Maze*, was praised for its anthropological, sociological, and historical interpretation of revolution, war, and peace in this region of the world.

In 1932, his book *Banana Gold*, based on his experiences in Honduras and Central America, was published. Like *Mexican Maze*, it was unusual in its depiction of patriotism and corruption. Indeed, the first-person point of view was used, giving the reader a personal account of what happened. Beals was more than an observer, he was a participant. Indeed, he used a personal style of reporting to describe the characters and milieu. In short, he presented slice-of-life experiences to the reader. Beals's descriptions were realistic and authentic. Only through description could the reader see what Beals witnessed.

The same year Beals traveled to Cuba to investigate the dictator Geraldo Machado. In 1933, *The Crime of Cuba* was published, in which Beals criticized Machado and the role of the United States. Machado was overthrown, and Beals became a hero to the young people of Cuba.

Beals later covered a general strike in Cuba for the North American Newspaper Alliance, then went to Louisiana to study Huey Long, the controversial governor of that state. He wrote *The Story of Huey P. Long*, which was published in 1935. In 1936, he served as a correspondent for the *New York Post*; he covered the Scottsboro trial in Alabama. Later, after the trial, he studied living conditions of sharecroppers.

Although he wrote fiction, his passion was traveling to a country and observing its people, including its politicians, then writing about it from a personal perspective.

Beals wrote his first autobiography in 1938. Titled *Glass Houses: Ten Years of Free-Lancing*, the book was insightful, to say the least. A second autobiography, *The Great Circle: Further Adventures in Free-Lancing*, was published in 1940.

For the remainder of his life, he lived primarily in the United States, although he visited other countries, particularly in Central and South America, as well as numerous islands in the Caribbean. Although he continued to write about other countries over the years, he also wrote several books about the history of Connecticut and New England.

In 1960, his book, *Brass-Knuckle Crusade: The Great Know-Nothing Conspiracy, 1820–1860*, was published. The book was well received by critics primarily because Beals had presented an insightful examination of party politics.

Beals died on June 26, 1979. He had written almost fifty books and had contributed numerous entries and chapters to others. However, he is remembered for his penetrating articles and books about various countries.

SELECTED WORKS

Brimstone and Chili: A Book of Personal Experiences in the Southwest and in Mexico (1927)
Mexican Maze (1931)
Banana Gold (1932)
The Crime of Cuba (1933)
Glass Houses: Ten Years of Free-Lancing (1938)
The Great Circle: Further Adventures in Free-Lancing (1940)
Brass Knuckle Crusade: The Great Know-Nothing Conspiracy, 1820–1860 (1960)

NOTE

1. Joan Cook, "Carlton Beals Dies; Correspondent, 85," *New York Times*, June 28, 1979, B15.

REFERENCES

Beals, Carleton. *Glass Houses: Ten Years of Free-Lancing*. Philadelphia: Lippincott, 1938.

———. *The Great Circle: Further Adventures in Free-Lancing*. Philadelphia: Lippincott, 1940.

Britton, John A. *Carleton Beals: A Radical Journalist in Latin America*. Albuquerque: University of New Mexico Press, 1987.

Sidney Bernard (1918–)

SIDNEY BERNARD WAS BORN ON FEBRUARY 4, 1918, in New York City. He served in the United States Army during World War II before he attended Columbia University. Leaving Columbia in 1947, he became a reporter for the Standard News Association. From the late 1950s to the early 1960s, he worked as a public relations writer for Fenster Associates, and from 1963 to 1967, he served as the New York editor for the *Literary Times*. When he left the *Times*, he became roving editor for the *Smith* and the *Newsletter* of New York City, for which he wrote entertaining, informative articles. He also wrote more than five hundred left-wing essays, articles, and poems for such magazines and newspapers as *Ramparts*, the *Realist*, the *Rogue*, the *National Observer*, the *New York Herald Tribune*, *Nation*, *Commonweal*, *Defiance*, and *Evergreen Review*, among others.

In 1969, a collection of Bernard's writing was published under the title *This Way to the Apocalypse: The 1960's*. Eight years later another collection was published. Titled *Witnessing: The Seventies*, the compilation contained essays that chronicled the previous nine years and concerned certain ideas and movements, especially various individuals and interesting places.

In 1984, Bernard wrote *Metamorphosis of Peace*.

SELECTED WORKS

This Way to the Apocalypse: The 1960's (1969)
Witnessing: The Seventies (1977)

REFERENCES

Bernard, Sidney. *This Way to the Apocalypse: The 1960's*. New York: Horizon, 1969.
———. *Witnessing: The Seventies*. New York: Horizon, 1977.

Ambrose Bierce
(1842–1914?)

AMBROSE BIERCE WAS A JOURNALIST who wrote sketches, columns, articles, and short stories. Born in Ohio in 1842, Bierce briefly attended the Kentucky Military Institute prior to the firing on Fort Sumter. Immediately, he volunteered for service and admirably served the Union. Indeed, he saw action on numerous fronts and was eventually wounded. He earned a commission and served on General Hazen's staff, drawing military maps. He marched through Georgia with General Sherman. Although he was taken prisoner in Alabama, he escaped within a few days.

When Bierce was released he worked for the Treasury Department, then for General Hazen, his old commanding officer, who was in charge of an expedition west. For almost a year he accompanied Hazen, surveying the territory. When Hazen sailed for Panama, Bierce remained in San Francisco, where he worked for the U.S. Sub-Treasury during the day. In the evening he wrote articles on politics and Poe-like short stories. His writing appeared in the *News-Letter* and *Alta California*. In 1868, he wrote editorial comments under "The Town Crier," a page filled with invective pieces and consequently enjoyed by the readers. Bierce used "The Town Crier" to present forcefully his scathing remarks. He attacked the ills of society as well as the rogues responsible. Through the *News-Letter*, he became a fixture in San Francisco, a position he readily accepted.

He moved to London in 1872, hoping to make his mark abroad. He wrote for a few magazines and, under the pseudonym of "Dod Grile," published *Fiend's Delight*, *Nuggets and Dust*, and *Cobwebs from an Empty Skull*.

When he returned to San Francisco a few years later, the city had changed. Hard times had set in. Dennis Kearney and his Workingmen's Party attributed the high unemployment among whites to the Chinese migrant workers, and unfortunately his prejudiced views were becoming popular. In response, Bierce published and edited the *Argonaut*, where perhaps his most famous column, "Prattle," was born. In this column, Bierce used wit to criticize every form of hypocrisy; consequently, he became a champion of causes in the eyes of San Franciscans. In addition, he wrote short stories, essays, and poetry. When his wife left him, he used his pen to belittle women. Men, too, were dissected and analyzed in almost every column; indeed, even simpletons and incompetents were brought before Bierce's scornful eyes and criticized.

Bierce sold the *Argonaut* in 1880 and moved to the Black Hills to manage a gold mine. Before the year ended, the company was bankrupt, and Bierce, having been refused a position with the *Argonaut*, was in desperate need of a job. Finally, his old column was accepted by the *Wasp*, a San Francisco weekly. Six years later, Bierce was approached by William Randolph Hearst, who enjoyed Bierce's column as well as his other writings. Hearst offered Bierce a position with the *San Francisco Examiner*, and "Prattle" remained there until the turn of the century. To say the least, the *Examiner* helped popularize Bierce's column as well as his short stories. In 1891, after he had written a number of stories about the Civil War, he published *Tales of Soldiers and Civilians*. Two years later he published *Can Such Things Be?*, a book of stories about the supernatural.

Bierce moved to Washington, D.C., in 1896 to report against an appropriations bill that was before Congress. If passed, the bill would have helped the Southern Pacific Railroad postpone loan repayments to the U.S. government. As a result of his accurate reports, as well as Hearst's power, the bill was defeated. Although he returned to San Francisco, he eventually talked Hearst into allowing him to move to Washington so that he could write more for the *New York Journal* and less for the *Examiner*. However, the column he produced, "The Passing Show," was nothing compared to "Prattle," and after a few years, Hearst put it in *Cosmopolitan*.

In 1912, Bierce published his *Collected Works*; he was seventy years old. He visited California, then journeyed to Tennessee to stand on the battlefields where he had fought and had witnessed numerous deaths. Heading southwest, he visited New Orleans, San Antonio, and El Paso, where he received credentials to enter Mexico. He had grown old and needed another battle to rejuvenate himself. In his last correspondence, he was with troops near Chihuahua. He was never seen again.

SELECTED WORKS

"The Town Crier" (newspaper column)
"Prattle" (newspaper column)

REFERENCES

Grenander, M. E. *Ambrose Bierce*. New York: Twayne, 1971.

McWilliams, Carey. *Ambrose Bierce: A Biography*. New York: Boni, 1929.

Morris, Roy. *Ambrose Bierce: Alone in Bad Company*. New York: Crown, 1995.

O'Connor, Richard. *Ambrose Bierce: A Biography*. Boston: Little, Brown, 1967.

Elias Boudinot
(1803–1839)

ELIAS BOUDINOT, A CHEROKEE INDIAN, advocated acculturation in the *Cherokee Phoenix*, a newspaper directed to Cherokees and whites.

Oo-watie, Boudinot's father, had taken advantage of the government's "civilization" program, which encouraged Cherokees to move away from traditional towns, and had left Hiwassee, Tennessee, and had settled with his wife, Susanna Reese, on a small farm at Oothcaloga in northwestern Georgia near the present-day town of Calhoun.

Gallegina or "Buck" (he later took the name "Elias Boudinot") was born in 1803 and was the first of nine children. His father enrolled him in the Moravian mission school at Spring Place, which had been accepting Cherokee children since 1804. Missionaries taught the children hoeing, chopping wood, weaving, cooking, plowing, sewing, and religion, linking the latter to civilization. As many children as possible were housed on the premises, primarily to prevent them from lapsing into "savage" ways.

Buck stayed at Spring Place until 1817. Elias Cornelius of the American Board of Commissioners for Foreign Missions invited Buck and several others from the mission to further their education at the American Board school in Cornwall, Connecticut. Buck and another boy accompanied Cornelius and Jeremiah Evarts on their return to New England. They visited Elias Boudinot, who had been a member of the Continental Congress and who advocated that the

American Indians were the lost tribes of Israel. Buck was impressed with Boudinot and enrolled in the American Board School as Elias Boudinot.

The school provided academic as well as practical instruction. Of course, religion was also emphasized, so that students could promote Christianity as well as practice a particular profession.

In 1820, Boudinot converted to Christianity. The American Board made arrangements for him to study at Andover Theological Seminary so that he could preach to the Cherokees in their language. His health prevented him from attending, however. In 1822, he returned to the Cherokee Nation, where he exhibited responsibility for the welfare of his people.

When Harriet Ruggles Gold asked her father for permission to marry Boudinot, her father refused. Interracial marriages, although some had occurred, were not socially acceptable. Harriet became critically ill soon after her father's decision; eventually, he changed his mind. Cornwall's citizens grew outraged. They blamed the American Board School for the interracial marriage. After all, if it had not been for the school, white female missionaries would not meet American Indians. The school soon closed, but Boudinot and Gold were married in 1826.

Boudinot continued to be an ardent advocate of "civilization." He believed that the progress of his people depended on the preservation of the Cherokees as a corporate group. Boudinot was a founder of and corresponding secretary for the Moral and Literary Society of the Cherokee Nation. He traveled to various cities and appealed for contributions, always prefacing his remarks with a summary of his people's accomplishments. His trips were a success. At least $1,500 was spent on a press, and Boudinot was offered the editorship of the *Cherokee Phoenix*, which he eventually accepted. Subscribers were found as far away as Mobile, Alabama, and Troy, New York.

The paper first appeared in 1827. Boudinot borrowed copy from other newspapers. He also published official correspondence and documents of the Cherokee Nation, legislation passed by the National Council, notices of weddings, meetings of societies, and advocating editorials. The paper became a powerful propaganda tool for the Cherokee Nation, and it demonstrated to whites the remarkable accomplishments of the Cherokees.

Although Boudinot mentioned the superior achievements of his people, he never implied that other tribes could not achieve the same.

In 1829, Boudinot changed the name of the newspaper to *The Cherokee Phoenix and Indians' Advocate*. The title reflected the editor's scope. Boudinot defended his people from certain whites, who criticized them or their progress. For instance, when the U.S. senator from Georgia claimed that the Cherokees were oppressed and exploited, Boudinot wrote an editorial that refuted his charges:

> Many of the people of the United States, who think with Mr. Forsyth that the Cherokee are *poor devils*, may be surprised to learn that among them are several societies for the spread of religion and morality, and what is still more astonishing, the chiefs of these people, "who grind the faces of the poor" and "keep them under, in poverty and ignorance," that "their avarice propensity may be gratified," generally take the lead and support them by their example and contributions. They have Missionary Societies, Tract Societies, Sunday School Societies, Benevolent Societies, Book Societies and Temperance Societies.[1]

Boudinot confronted charges and accusations. Some whites refused to believe that an Indian could edit a newspaper, for instance. Boudinot assured them that the paper was published by an Indian for Indians and whites. Boudinot also published Cherokee judicial proceedings for the purpose of enlightening whites, who sometimes were reluctant in sentencing their own when they committed similar crimes.

The Cherokees were portrayed in the paper as a "civilized" people because Boudinot believed that the Cherokee Nation was progressing; he also realized that if whites considered Cherokees savages, they might exterminate American Indians.

In 1828, the state of Georgia annexed a large section of Cherokee territory. As a result, that part of the Nation came under the state. The National Council was prohibited from convening, and

Indians could not mine gold discovered on Cherokee land near Dahlonega.

Whites flooded the Nation in search of gold and seized Cherokee property. Cherokee laws were not considered valid by the state of Georgia, and Boudinot criticized the Georgia legislature. Federal troops were sent in by President Andrew Jackson to maintain peace; then the governor of Georgia sent in the Georgia Guard. Members of this unit harassed the Indians. Boudinot reported on various encounters between the Cherokees and members of the Georgia Guard, even criticizing the latter. He was brought before the commander for printing "lies." Because he could prove that the articles were true, however, he was not arrested.

The Indian Removal Act was passed in 1830. This piece of legislation empowered the president to negotiate Indian removal. Treaty commissioners arrived in the Cherokee Nation soon after and faced a cold reception.

In 1831, Boudinot toured the United States to raise funds for the newspaper and the Nation. He returned about six months later, in 1832.

Several months later he signed a petition that favored removal. When his views became apparent to members of the Cherokee government, they prohibited him from expressing them in the paper. Boudinot resigned as editor the same year.

Three years, later Boudinot and several other Cherokees signed the Treaty of New Echota, which negotiated an exchange of Cherokee land in the Southeast for territory in the West (now the state of Oklahoma). This action, which would have saved the Cherokee Nation, was not accepted by the elite class that governed the Cherokee Nation. Boudinot was seen as a traitor rather than a patriot by most Cherokees. Indeed, they charged that he sought to destroy rather than save the Nation.

Chief John Ross and other leaders of the Nation attacked Boudinot and vice versa, until Ross realized that the settlement under the provisions of the treaty could be increased.

The Senate ratified the treaty in 1836; the Cherokees had two years to move. Although hundreds of Cherokees believed Chief

John Ross would make it possible for them to remain, they were forced to leave their land in 1838.

Boudinot's wife died in 1836. He married Delight Sargent, a missionary, in 1837, and they moved to the new Cherokee Nation before the mass migration.

In 1839, Boudinot was building a house when several Cherokees approached and requested medicine. They attacked him with knives and tomahawks, and he died soon after.

SELECTED WORKS

Cherokee Phoenix (editor)
The Cherokee Phoenix and Indians' Advocate (editor)

NOTE

1. *Cherokee Phoenix*, October 8, 1830.

REFERENCES

Dale, Edward Everett, and Gaston Litton, eds. *Cherokee Cavaliers: Forty Years of Cherokee History as Told in the Correspondence of the Ridge-Watie-Boudinot Family*. Norman: University of Oklahoma Press, 1939.

Gabriel, Ralph Henry. *Elias Boudinot, Cherokee, & His America*. Norman: University of Oklahoma Press, 1941.

Gaul, Theresa Strouth, ed. *To Marry an Indian: The Marriage of Harriett Gold and Elias Boudinot in Letters, 1823–1839*. Chapel Hill: University of North Carolina Press, 2005.

Perdue, Theda, ed. *Cherokee Editor: The Writings of Elias Boudinot*. Knoxville: University of Tennessee Press, 1983.

Heywood Broun
(1888-1939)

BORN IN 1888 IN BROOKLYN, newspaper columnist Heywood Broun attended Harvard University for four years, but he failed to graduate primarily because of his grades in French. When he left the campus in 1910, he joined the staff of the *New York Morning Telegraph*, a newspaper he had worked for during the summer of 1908. Two years later, he asked for an increase in salary and was dismissed.

Broun became a sports writer for the *New York Tribune*. Broun mixed excitement with facts, which allowed readers to experience the event as if they had been sitting in the stands.

Eventually Broun served as the newspaper's drama critic. In 1917, he was one of the newspaper's war correspondents in France, where his critical dispatches about the United States military were sometimes censored. When the war ended, he returned to the *Tribune* as drama critic and began a column on books and authors that not only expressed his opinions but captured hundreds of readers. Consequently, in 1921, he was lured to the *New York World* and began the column for which he is known—"It Seems to Me," in which he presented his opinions on major issues. The column was severely criticized by certain prominent members of New York City society, particularly when he demanded that Eugene Debs be released from prison. Broun demanded equal justice for all. When he vehemently attacked Governor Alvan T. Fuller's and Harvard president Abbott Lawrence Lowell's recommendations not to allow

Nicola Sacco and Bartolomeo Vanzetti a new trial, Ralph Pulitzer, the *World*'s editor and publisher, demanded that he write on another topic. Broun refused, and Pulitzer suspended him. Broun was not deterred, however. In an article for the *Nation*, he criticized the *World* for its reverse philosophy and lack of responsibility. Of course, after the article appeared, Broun was no longer wanted by the *World*. Because he was an excellent and insightful writer, however, he was hired by Roy W. Howard's *New York Telegram*, which eventually purchased the *World*. The Scripps-Howard *World-Telegram* published and syndicated Broun's columns until 1939, when Broun complained of how some of his columns had been altered or deleted.

In addition to his column for the *World-Telegram*, Broun wrote another for the *Nation* and then for the *New Republic*. He also helped organize the American Newspaper Guild in 1933.

"Sacco and Vanzetti," one of Broun's most bitter columns, exhibited a style that was direct and emphatic. With the quotation "It is death condemning life!" Broun began his argument. Sacco and Vanzetti stood out in society; thus, they had to be killed. They were life, and those who killed them were death. Broun argued that what happened in the courtroom, specifically the sentencing, was not an isolated ruling. Rather, in the American system of justice, particularly when American jurors judged defendants of another country or race, prejudices interfered much too often. Broun condemned not only the system but certain individuals such as Governor Fuller who had the courtroom and subsequently the verdict in their hands. Broun questioned whether those in high places should have the power to condemn others.

Broun's form of advocacy journalism was more inclusive, thought-provoking, and literary than other forms of advocacy journalism practiced at the time. Broun, who could criticize as well as praise a position, a decision, or an individual, had few rivals.

Broun died of pneumonia in 1939.

SELECTED WORK

"It Seems to Me" (newspaper column)

REFERENCES

Kramer, Dale. *Heywood Broun: A Biographical Portrait.* New York: Current Books, 1949.

O'Connor, Richard. *Heywood Broun: A Biography.* New York: Putnam, 1975.

William F. Buckley Jr. (1925–2008)

CONSERVATIVE EDITOR, COLUMNIST, best-selling author, and television host, William F. Buckley Jr. was born to William Frank and Aloise Buckley in New York City in 1925. His parents were Roman Catholic and wealthy. As a child, he attended private schools in England and France. When he returned to the United States, he attended the Millbrook School in New York, where he prepared for college. Upon graduation in 1943, he entered the University of Mexico. After a semester, he entered the U.S. Army and served in the infantry during World War II. Although he attained the rank of second lieutenant, Buckley realized that a career in the military was not for him. Consequently, when he was released in 1946, he attended Yale University, where he studied economics, history, and political science and developed a strong interest in the university's newspaper and forensics team.

Buckley received his bachelor's degree in 1950 but remained at the university as an instructor in Spanish. A year later he wrote the controversial book *God and Man at Yale: The Superstitions of Academic Freedom*, which attacked the anti-Christian, proliberal ideas taught by certain faculty members at Yale. Buckley's book caused a stir among reviewers. Some believed that Buckley was naive; others believed that he was incorrect in his assessment. Buckley left Yale and worked for a year as an agent for the Central Intelligence Agency.

In 1952, Buckley became an associate editor of the *American Mercury*, an iconoclastic magazine founded by H. L. Mencken and George Nathan in 1924. The magazine was sold to several people, one of whom was Clendenin J. Ryan. Ryan's editor, William Bradford Huie, an archconservative who enjoyed exposés, purchased the publication from Ryan and then sold it to J. Russell Maguire in 1952. Huie, however, remained editor until Maguire's anti-Semitic philosophy caused him to resign. Buckley resigned, too, and worked during the next several years as a freelance writer. In 1954, he collaborated with his brother-in-law, L. Brent Bozell, on *McCarthy and His Enemies*, which defended what McCarthy and men like him had tried to accomplish in American society. A year later he raised almost $300,000 from friends and launched the largest-selling periodical devoted to conservatism, the *National Review*. Primarily a journal of political essays, Buckley's publication became the most important periodical on the American Right. Indeed, Buckley recruited such writers and editors as John Chamberlain, Frank Chodorov, L. Brent Bozell, Suzanne La Follette, Max Eastman, Whittaker Chambers, Priscilla Buckley, Russell Kirk, James Burnham, Ralph de Toledano, Joan Didion, Frank Meyer, Renata Adler, Eugene Lyons, Garry Wills, and John Leonard.

The publication received considerable criticism. Certain critics claimed that it was not truly conservative. Nonetheless, the *National Review* surpassed the circulation of its liberal competitors the *Nation* and the *New Republic* by a sufficient margin. In 1957, approximately sixteen thousand copies per issue were published. In 1980, the number of copies had increased to almost one hundred thousand per issue.

Buckley devoted time to the periodical, but his desire to write books continued. In 1959, for instance, he wrote *Up from Liberalism*, in which he denounced liberalism and its ruination of society.

In the 1960s, Buckley initiated or was a proponent in initiating several conservative activities. In 1960, for example, he helped establish Young Americans for Freedom, which was organized to attract young conservatives. A year later, together with other conservatives, he formed the New York Conservative Party. In 1962, he began a syndicated newspaper column that was written for the sole purpose of presenting his conservative points of view on major issues. The column, filled with wit as well as information, attracted thousands of readers of some 350 newspapers by 1990. In 1966, the weekly program *Firing Line*, on which Buckley discussed with guests a sociological or political issue, aired on WOR-TV. Five years later the Public Broadcasting System purchased the program, and Buckley became a national celebrity.

Buckley, who devoutly supported such political figures as Senator Barry Goldwater, Richard Nixon, and Ronald Reagan, was appointed by President Nixon in 1969 to the five-member advisory board of the U.S. Information Agency. He resigned in 1972, however, when he disagreed with the Nixon administration's policies toward the agency. In 1974, in the aftermath of Watergate, he, together with his brother, Senator James L. Buckley, another conservative, called for the president's resignation for the good of the nation.

Buckley, who wrote in the 1960s against the extreme right-wing organization called the John Birch Society, also condemned wage and price controls, American-Chinese relations, détente with the Soviet Union, abortion, the welfare state, and injustice. His articles for the *National Review, Esquire, Harper's, Saturday Review,* and *Atlantic Monthly,* among others, were collected and published in several volumes in the 1960s and 1970s. For instance, *Execution Eve and Other Contemporary Ballads,* which was filled with political satire, was published in 1975. *A Hymnal: The Controversial Arts* was published in 1978 and, like the previous book, contained columns and essays that promoted the conservative spirit or chastised the liberals.

In 1976, Buckley wrote his first successful spy novel, *Saving the Queen,* which combined an intriguing story with his conservative propaganda. The hero, Blackford Oakes, appeared in other novels, including *Last Call for Blackford Oakes,* which was published in 2005.

Buckley also presented his personal life in several books. For instance, in 1971, he wrote *Cruising Speed: A Documentary*, which reported a typical week in a diary-like format—from his numerous activities to the social functions in which he found himself. *Overdrive: A Personal Documentary*, which was published in 1983, was similar. He also discussed his fascination with sailing by chronicling three expeditions in *Airborne: A Sentimental Journey*, *Atlantic High: A Celebration*, and *Racing through Paradise: A Pacific Passage*, which were published in 1976, 1982, and 1987, respectively. In 1997, he wrote about his Catholic faith as well as about the American culture in *Nearer, My God: An Autobiography of Faith*.

In addition to writing books about conservative politics, Buckley edited several, including *Keeping the Tablets: Modern American Conservative Thought*, which was published in 1988 and was a revision of *Did You Ever See a Dream Walking? American Conservative Thought in the Twentieth Century* that was published in 1970.

In 1986, Buckley examined Mexico, Poland, and Spain, as well as certain figures such as Karl Marx, Pope Paul VI, and Henry Kissinger, in the compilation *Right Reason*. Four years later, he outlined five reasons for a national program for young people in *Gratitude: Reflections on What We Owe to Our Country*. Buckley believed that this program would (1) help build character, (2) allow youth to repay a social debt, (3) mix the various classes of society in a common endeavor, (4) provide needed services, and (5) salvage those less fortunate.

A collection of columns, essays, and other writings that opened windows on history was published in 1993. Titled *Happy Days Were Here Again: Reflections of a Libertarian Journalist*, the collection's articles were divided into attitudinal categories such as "Assailing," "Playing," and "Celebrating" and concerned such luminaries as Jesse Jackson, Mario Cuomo, John Kenneth Galbraith, Carl Sagan, and others.

Buckley continued to practice advocacy journalism to promote his conservative views in the 1990s; however, it was his magazine that allowed others to advocate certain conservative beliefs.

In 1999, he wrote the novel *The Redhunter: A Novel Based on the Life of Senator Joe McCarthy*, which concerned the senator's search for Communists in the United States. The novel was criticized for presenting only one side of the story.

A year later *Let Us Talk of Many Things: The Collected Speeches of William F. Buckley Jr.* was published and contained a sampling of the speeches that he had delivered during the last several decades.

In 2004, in *Miles Gone By: A Literary Autobiography*, Buckley examined himself and his friends.

William F. Buckley Jr. died on February 27, 2008, in his home in Connecticut.

SELECTED WORKS

National Review (founder)
"On the Right" (newspaper column)
God and Man at Yale: The Superstitions of "Academic Freedom" (1951)
Up from Liberalism (1959)
Rumbles Left and Right: A Book about Troublesome People and Ideas (1963)
The Jeweler's Eye: A Book of Irresistible Political Reflections (1968)
The Governor Listeth: A Book of Inspired Political Revelations (1970)
Inveighing We Will Go (1972)
Execution Eve and Other Contemporary Ballads (1975)
Right Reason (1985)
Happy Days Were Here Again: Reflections of a Libertarian Journalist (1993)

REFERENCES

Buckley, William F., Jr. *Nearer, My God: An Autobiography of Faith*. New York: Doubleday, 1997.

———. *Miles Gone By: A Literary Autobiography*. Washington, D.C.: Regnery, 2004.

Judis, John. *William F. Buckley, Jr.: Patron Saint of the Conservatives*. New York: Simon & Schuster, 1988.

Markmann, Charles L. *The Buckleys: A Family Examined*. New York: Morrow, 1973.

John Jay Chapman
(1862-1933)

JOHN JAY CHAPMAN WAS PRIMARILY an advocate who wrote critical essays on politics and society's mores. He also wrote essays about prominent writers.

Chapman was born to Eleanor and Henry Chapman, a successful stockbroker who became president of the New York Stock Exchange, in New York City in 1862. Chapman attended St. Paul's School in Concord, New Hampshire, where he held to the religious rituals of the place to the extent that other boys thought he was odd. Eventually his parents removed him from the school.

Chapman ultimately attended Harvard, from which he graduated in 1885. He traveled throughout Europe for a year. When he returned home, he met Minna Timmins, whom he fought over at a social function. Chapman, who temporarily disregarded his religious convictions, beat the man who had been courting Minna and later, because of guilt, burned his own left hand, which had to be amputated. Chapman married Minna in 1889.

Chapman and his bride lived in New York City, where they started a family. Chapman practiced law, which he disliked, and started writing essays about literature, including an examination of Dante's *Inferno* as well as Shakespeare's works. In addition, he grew interested in politics. As a result, he became president of the Good Government Club, which had been founded by Edmond Kelly for the purpose of fighting Tammany Hall and had drawn on the membership of the City Reform Club. Chapman had been a member of the latter for several years. According to Edmund Wilson, "Chapman and another Harvard man assumed the leadership of the Good Government movement, and from 1895 through 1900 he had an odd and very interesting career as a non-socialist political radical."[1]

Chapman campaigned against Tammany and in the process spoke against Joseph Choate and Edwin Godkin of the *New York Evening Post*. Chapman became one of the leaders of the Independent Party.

In 1897, Chapman's wife died. Perhaps to take his mind off his loss he started *The Political Nursery*, a monthly publication in which he discussed the political issues of the day. In 1898, he married Elizabeth Chanler. The same year he and others persuaded Theodore Roosevelt to allow the party to nominate him for the governorship of New York. Roosevelt accepted the offer, but he reneged when Tom Platt, the leader of the Republicans, offered the Republican ticket to him. According to Wilson, "He observed that Roosevelt presently persuaded himself that he had never understood the original proposal and that he thereafter became very vociferous over the damage done progressive movements by fanatics on their 'lunatic fringe.'"[2]

Chapman used *The Political Nursery* to attack Roosevelt, among other politicians, who had represented the Independents. The review lasted until January 1901.

In 1898, a collection of his essays entitled *Emerson, and Other Essays*—which critiqued the popular writers of the day, including Ralph Waldo Emerson, Robert Louis Stevenson, and Walt Whitman, among others—was published. The same year Chapman published *Causes and Consequences*, which criticized the absurd relationship between business and government. Indeed, Chapman believed that businesses had too much influence on politicians and politics and consequently had changed the American political system and the country's culture. In 1900, he published *Practical Agitation*, which declared that political reformation was only possible when society changed. Chapman believed that in order for society to change, one had to change his or her personal life. Basically, he proclaimed morality.

After the latter book was published, Chapman suffered from grippe and was bedridden for a year. Insecurity set in, and when he was able to leave his bed, he required crutches.

For two years, until his young son drowned while the family vacationed in Austria, he carelessly put life aside. Perhaps it was the tragedy or it was the psychological help he received from William James that made him realize that life was to be lived. At any rate, he recovered and lived for the most part at his country home.

In 1908, he published *Four Plays for Children*. Two years later he published *The Treason and Death of Benedict Arnold: A Play for a Greek Theatre*, which was for adults. The same year another collection of essays, *Learning and Other Essays*, was published.

Chapman became an abolitionist and held a service in Coatesville, Pennsylvania, in 1912 for an African American who had been tortured and burned to death a year earlier. Although his speech was filled with love, few heard it.

In 1913, he published *William Lloyd Garrison*, a book of essays about Garrison, an abolitionist who, on more than one occasion, employed violent action against slavery, which Garrison deemed evil.

A year later Chapman and his wife visited Victor, his son, who was studying in Paris, not realizing that Victor would die in World War I two years later. When Victor died, Chapman seemed to lose his desire to write. Although he had published three collections of essays—*Greek Genius, and Other Essays, Memories and Milestones,* and *Notes on Religion*—in 1915, it was several years before he produced another book of any significance.

In 1922, he published a collection of essays about Shakespeare under the title *A Glance toward Shakespeare*. He published a collection of essays about religion under the title *Letters and Religion* two years later. Although he published several collections of essays about literature, one of his last collections of essays appeared under the title *New Horizons in American Life* in 1932. The essays concerned higher education in the United States.

Chapman died several days after an operation in 1933.

SELECTED WORKS

The Political Nursery (founder)
Emerson, and Other Essays (1898)
Causes and Consequences (1898)
Practical Agitation (1900)

NOTES

1. Edmund Wilson, "John Jay Chapman," *The Triple Thinkers: Ten Essays on Literature* (New York: Harcourt, Brace, 1938), 170.
2. Wilson, "John Jay Chapman," 172–173.

REFERENCES

Bernstein, Melvin Herbert. *John Jay Chapman*. New York: Twayne, 1964.
Hovey, Richard B. *John Jay Chapman, an American Mind*. New York: Columbia University Press, 1959.

(Leroy) Eldridge Cleaver (1935–1998)

ELDRIDGE CLEAVER WAS BORN IN WABBASEKA, Arkansas, in 1935. His father, Leroy Cleaver, worked as a waiter and piano player in a nightclub; his mother was an elementary school teacher. When his father got a job as a waiter on the Super Chief, a train running between Chicago and Los Angeles, the family moved to Phoenix, Arizona, one of the cities in which the train stopped.

Cleaver shined shoes when he was not in school. The job lasted about two years, until the family moved to Watts, a section of Los Angeles. His parents separated shortly thereafter, and Cleaver eventually was arrested for stealing a bicycle. He was sent to the Fred C. Nelles School for Boys in Whittier, California. Cleaver learned about crime from others. When he was released in 1953, he sold marijuana and was sent to another reform school. Cleaver failed to learn from his mistakes, however. Several days after his release, he was arrested for possession of marijuana. He was sentenced to the state penitentiary at Soledad, where he read works by Thomas Paine, Richard Wright, Voltaire, Karl Marx, Lenin, and Mikhail Bakunin, to mention a few. Cleaver also analyzed his predicament as well as that of African American men in general. He had assumed that since the law had been written by whites for whites, it had not applied to him. Now, he looked at white America through new eyes. As he wrote in *Soul on Ice*, "Somehow I arrived at the conclusion that, as a matter of principle, it was of paramount

51

importance for me to have an antagonistic, ruthless attitude toward white women."[1] He considered himself to be an "outlaw" because he "had stepped outside of the white man's law," which he "repudiated with scorn."

Cleaver was finally released after two and a half years. He sold marijuana and then became a rapist. First, he raped African American girls who lived in the ghetto. Then he sought white women. As he wrote, "It delighted me that I was defying and trampling upon the white man's law, upon his system of values, and that I was defiling his women—and this point, I believe, was the most satisfying to me because I was very resentful over the historical fact of how the white man has used the black woman. I felt I was getting revenge."[2]

Within a year, Cleaver was arrested and sentenced to serve two to fourteen years. He was sent to San Quentin and then transferred to Folsom. Cleaver examined his actions and admitted that he was wrong. He could not approve the act of rape and wrote, "I lost my self-respect. My pride as a man dissolved and my whole fragile moral structure seemed to collapse."[3] He started writing primarily to save himself. Concurrently, he learned about Elijah Muhammad, who headed the Black Muslims, and the Black Muslim movement. Cleaver was converted and spent numerous hours reading the Bible. Later, he followed Malcolm X, who had separated from Elijah Muhammad. When Cleaver learned about Malcolm's assassination, he defended his ideas and urged other inmates to support Malcolm's beliefs.

In 1963, Cleaver wrote his first letter to Beverly Axelrod, a lawyer, to ask her to handle his case. This letter began one of the most discussed love stories via letters in recent history. Axelrod responded to his letters and, after meeting him, became a devoted friend who encouraged the owner and editor of *Ramparts* magazine to examine some of what Eldridge had written. In June 1966, Edward Keating published Cleaver's essay "Notes on a Native Son," in which he criticized the work of James Baldwin, particularly the homosexuality theme that permeated *Notes of a Native Son*. Other articles by Cleaver appeared in the ensuing issues. As a result of his affiliation with *Ramparts* as well as the support he received from the intellectual elite, he was paroled in November 1966.

Cleaver worked for *Ramparts* and was one of the founders of Black House, which appealed to youngsters interested in learning about black culture. In early 1967, he met Huey Newton and Bobby Seale, who founded the Black Panthers, a militant organization based in Oakland, California. He joined the organization shortly thereafter, primarily to protect African Americans from being harassed by police.

In October 1967, a police officer was killed when violence erupted between the Black Panthers and the police. Huey Newton was arrested and sentenced for manslaughter. Cleaver, who had not touched a weapon, was not charged, but in April 1968, another confrontation between the police and the Black Panthers occurred. Bobby Hutton, a young Black Panther, was killed, and Cleaver was wounded. He was sent to jail, but he only had to serve two months.

In the fall of 1968, Cleaver lectured on racism at the University of California at Berkeley. Later, he was the Peace and Freedom Party's presidential candidate and received thirty thousand votes. On November 27, 1968, he was ordered to return to jail, but he fled the country. He lived in or visited Cuba, Algeria, France, the Soviet Union, China, North Korea, and North Vietnam. While overseas, he was interviewed by reporters of *Time*, the *Washington Post*, and other magazines and newspapers.

After about eight years, in 1975, Cleaver returned to the United States to face prosecution. By pleading guilty to an assault charge, he was sentenced to 1,200 hours of community service. The system that he had despised was extremely lenient to him. Cleaver had changed, and his rhetoric was no longer espousing hate. As he explained to one reporter, "I found the systems of dictatorships and communism to be absolutely unacceptable. Living in those countries put an end to my advocacy of communism."[4] In 1982, he became a Mormon. Critics complained that he had sold out. Rather than being an activist, he had become a pacifist. Even his book *Soul on Fire*, which had appeared in 1978, was severely criticized for its languid style and syrupy subject matter. Many critics longed for the old Eldridge Cleaver, the one who would bite; they were not amused by the new one.

Cleaver ran as a conservative candidate for Congress in 1984 but was not successful. During the late 1980s, he earned money from lecturing, making and selling ceramic objects, and writing. However, in 1987, he was arrested for having cocaine. A year later he was arrested for stealing. His marriage ended in divorce after a long separation.

Although Huey Newton was killed by a drug dealer in 1989, Cleaver and Bobby Seale toured the country, speaking on college and university campuses about the Black Panthers. However, he underwent brain surgery after receiving a head injury in 1994. His health began to fail while living in a halfway house in Pomona, California. He died in 1998.

Cleaver's book *Soul on Ice* was a personal indictment of the white man's world, and it revealed quite candidly how one African American got caught in a system that he could not understand, let alone respect or appreciate. Perhaps no other book captured the animosity that many African Americans felt toward whites as well as this one, and Cleaver's personal style added punch to each indictment discussed.

SELECTED WORKS

Soul on Ice (1968)
Soul on Fire (1978)

NOTES

1. Eldridge Cleaver, *Soul on Ice* (New York: McGraw-Hill, 1968), 13.
2. Cleaver, *Soul on Ice*, 14.
3. Cleaver, *Soul on Ice*, 15.
4. "Whatever Happened to . . . Eldridge Cleaver," *Ebony* (March 1988), 66.

References

Cleaver, Eldridge. *Eldridge Cleaver: Post-prison Writings and Speeches*. Ed. Robert Scheer. New York: Random House, 1969.

———. *Soul on Fire*. Waco, Tex.: Word Books, 1978.

———. *Target Zero: A Life in Writing*. Ed. Kathleen Cleaver. New York: Palgrave Macmillan, 2006.

Rout, Kathleen. *Eldridge Cleaver*. Boston: Twayne, 1991.

George Creel
(1876–1953)

GEORGE CREEL WAS BORN ON DECEMBER 1, 1876, to Virginia and Henry Creel in Lafayette County, Missouri. His father was generally unemployed and drunk. His mother supported the family by sewing for others and running a boarding house. Creel attended public schools, including one year of high school, which he disliked. He quit and eventually wandered through the Southwest.

When he was twenty, he was hired as a reporter by the *Kansas City World*. However, when Creel was assigned a story and failed to deliver, he was fired. He journeyed to New York City, where he was rejected by every newspaper. He earned money by shoveling snow and selling newspapers. He also wrote jokes, some of which were sold to William Randolph Hearst's *New York Evening Journal*, as well as *Judge* and *Puck*, among other publications.

In 1898, he was offered a staff position at the *New York American*, which he accepted. He wrote humor for the paper and contributed similar jokes to the *New York Evening Journal*. Soon he tried to enlist in the campaigns in Cuba and the Philippines but was not accepted.

Arthur Grissom, a friend who had married a wealthy young woman, offered Creel a position with a new publication in Kansas City. Creel accepted, and the *Kansas City Independent* appeared in 1899. Filled with editorials, social and political news, and stories about sports, the paper offered readers a weekly journal of opinion.

However, Grissom, who went to New York City to start the *Smart Set*, left Creel the financially weak journal. Creel was influenced by Henry George's single-tax idea and soon supported the Democratic Party. Unfortunately, Kansas City had two Democratic factions, one headed by Thomas Pendergast and one headed by Frank Walsh and Joe Shannon. Creel opposed the faction headed by Pendergast. He supported Joseph Folk, a Democratic reformer, for governor of Missouri. He also wrote about social issues, including the rights of women. He advocated for laws that would protect workers. He supported public ownership of utilities and the commission form of government. He advocated for the single tax. He advocated against prostitution.

Although he continued publishing the weekly, procuring enough advertisements to pay for the publication was difficult. Finally, after ten years, he left the weekly when he was offered a position to write editorials for the *Denver Post*. Creel wrote articles for the paper, but he did not have editorial control, which he had expected. He confronted Fred Bonfils and Harry Tammen, the paper's owners, and Bonfils persuaded him to stay. Creel advocated for a commission form of government and public ownership of utilities. He supported the city's efforts to purchase the water company, but eleven state senators blocked it. Creel attacked the senators, stating they were traitors. He also suggested that they be lynched. One of the senators sued for libel, but Creel won in court and continued writing advocating editorials for the paper, including one in which he mentioned the names of politicians he strongly supported. However, before the editorial saw print, Bonfils and Tammen substituted the names with names of other politicians who Creel had not supported.

Creel resigned and moved to New York City in 1911, where he wrote for *Cosmopolitan*. For assignments, he traveled to Mississippi and Ohio to interview politicians. Then he traveled to Colorado, where he was offered a position with the *Rocky Mountain News*, which he accepted. Creel wrote editorials that opposed Robert W. Speer, the mayor of Denver who removed people he did not like from office.

Creel married Blanche Bates, an actress, in 1912, the year he became police commissioner. Henry Arnold, who Creel had supported, had become mayor. However, when Creel reminded Arnold about his campaign promises, Arnold put the police under the fire commissioner, whom Creel considered a drunk. Eventually, Arnold dismissed Creel.

Creel and his wife moved to New York City, where he wrote investigative articles for *Harper's Weekly*, *Everybody's*, and other publications. Creel, together with Judge Benjamin Lindsey and Edwin Markham, wrote *Children of Bondage*, which critically examined child labor, in 1914.

In 1916, Creel supported President Woodrow Wilson and became part of his reelection campaign. In addition to organizing a committee of authors who supported Wilson, he wrote articles that appeared in newspapers and the book *Wilson and the Issues*, which explained and defended the president's foreign policies and social reforms.

Wilson won reelection. In 1917, after the United States had entered World War I, he appointed Creel chairman of the Committee on Public Information (CPI). As chairman, Creel oversaw a committee that was devoted to spreading propaganda about the United States and the war. Indeed, the committee generated six thousand press releases, millions of pamphlets, and the *Official Bulletin*, which was a daily newspaper, among other publications. It also supported seventy-five thousand speakers. However, Creel and the committee were not without their critics. He insulted members of the U.S. Congress as well as members of the president's administration. Although the press demanded that he be fired, Wilson kept him but told him to keep his mouth shut about members of Congress and his administration.

When the president traveled to the Paris Peace Conference in 1919, Creel joined him. However, after the war, the CPI ceased to exist, and Creel became a writer for *Collier's*. In addition to writing articles, he wrote books. For instance, he wrote *How We Advertised America*, which was published in 1920 and discussed the CPI's efforts during World War I. *The War, the World and Wilson*, which was published the same year, examined the president's Fourteen Points and the League of Nations.

In 1926, Creel and his family moved to San Francisco, where he continued to write. For instance, he examined the nationalism of Mexico in *People Next Door: An Interpretive History of Mexico and the Mexicans*. A year later *Sons of the Eagle: Soaring Figures from America's Past*, a collection of previously published articles about historical personalities, was published. In 1932, he published *Tom Paine—Liberty Bell*, which concerned another historical personality.

In the 1930s, Creel supported Franklin D. Roosevelt and his New Deal policies. In 1933, he worked for the National Recovery Administration. A year later, he sought the Democratic nomination for governor of California, but lost. He accepted a position with *Collier's*, then worked briefly for the Works Progress Administration. In the late 1930s, Roosevelt appointed him to the Golden Gate International Exposition in San Francisco.

Creel's wife, Blanche, died in 1941. They had two children. Creel married Alice Rosseter in 1943. However, she died in 1948. Creel tried to reprise his role as an instrument of propaganda for the government during World War II, but he was rejected.

His book *War Criminals and Punishment*, in which he claimed that Germany and Japan should be severely punished, was published in 1944. Three years later, he wrote the memoir, *Rebel at Large: Recollections of Fifty Crowded Years*. Creel believed that Lenin and Trotsky were agents of Germany. He thought President Harry S. Truman had ties to Thomas Pendergast's political faction in Kansas City. In 1949, *Russia's Race of Asia* was published. In this book, Creel claimed that the Communists in China were merely puppets of the former Soviet Union.

Creel died in San Francisco in 1953.

SELECTED WORKS

Children in Bondage (with Benjamin Lindsey and Edwin Markham, 1914)
Chivalry Versus Justice: Why the Women of the Nation Demand the Right to Vote (1915)
Wilson and the Issues (1916)

The War, the World and Wilson (1920)
How We Advertised America (1920)
War Criminals and Punishment (1944)
Russia's Race for Asia (1949)

REFERENCES

Chenery, William L. *So It Seemed*. New York: Harcourt, Brace, 1952.
Creel, George. *Rebel at Large: Recollections of Fifty Crowded Years*. New York: Putnam's, 1947.
Lansing, Robert. *War Memoirs of Robert Lansing*. Indianapolis: Bobbs-Merrill, 1935.
Mock, James R., and Cedric Larson. *Words That Won the War*. Princeton, N.J.: Princeton University Press, 1939.

Midge Decter (1927-)

BORN IN ST. PAUL IN 1927 to Rose and Harry Rosenthal, a merchant, Midge Decter graduated from Central High School. She attended the University of Minnesota for a year and then transferred to the Jewish Theological Seminary of America in New York City, which she attended from 1946 to 1948 without receiving a degree.

She married Moshe Decter in 1947. However, this marriage ended in divorce seven years later. Decter became a secretary in the offices of *Commentary*, the American Jewish Committee's prestigious magazine. Two years later, in 1956, she married Norman Podhoretz and became an assistant editor at *Midstream*. This position, which she held until 1958, was extremely beneficial to her. As an assistant editor, she learned the mechanics of the magazine industry.

Decter's husband became editor of *Commentary* in 1960, and she joined the magazine as managing editor a year later. In addition, she contributed articles that vituperatively discussed women's liberation. Indeed, Decter believed that the goal of feminists was freedom from all responsibility.

In 1962, Decter left *Commentary*, and for the next three years she did not work in the magazine industry. Instead, she became an editor at the Hudson Institute's national security and social issues research center. In 1966, she started hopping from one job to another. By 1973, she had worked at CBS Legacy Books, *Harper's*,

61

and *Saturday Review/World*. In 1974, she became a senior editor at Basic Books. She resigned from this position in 1980 to begin the Committee for the Free World. She ended the committee after the Soviet Union collapsed. From 1991 until 1995, she served as a distinguished fellow at the Institute on Religion and Public Life. She served as a member at several think tank organizations, including the Heritage Foundation and the Hoover Institution.

Decter's first book, *The Liberated Woman and Other Americans*, a collection of critical essays that had appeared in such periodicals as *Harper's*, the *New York Review*, the *Atlantic*, *Commentary*, *Book Week*, and *Partisan Review*, was published in 1970. Reviewed by prominent critics from coast to coast, the book immediately propelled the author into national attention because of its controversial, rather conservative stance on the feminist movement.

Criticized by some, praised by others, Decter's second effort, *The New Chastity and Other Arguments against Women's Liberation*, which appeared in 1972, was extremely critical of the feminist movement. Indeed, she asserted that the women's movement had not helped women in their careers. According to Decter, the women's movement had stifled women's efforts by refusing to acknowledge the new freedoms, including birth control.

In 1975, in her third book, *Liberal Parents, Radical Children*, Decter ridiculed the youth of the 1960s and 1970s for not accepting responsibilities and for not facing the adult world. She placed the cause for young people's indifference on their parents, who she maintained were ultimately responsible. To Decter, parents had been too permissive and had failed to show authority. The book was severely criticized by some reviewers.

In 2001, *An Old Wife's Tale: My Seven Decades in Love and War* was published. To a certain extent, this was Decter's memoir, since she presented details about her personal life—from being reared in Minnesota, to attending college, to working in New York City. In addition, she examined her brief marriage to Decter and her lengthy marriage to Podhoretz. However, she also presented her political and social views, especially her views toward feminism. Needless to say, some reviewers praised her analysis of the subject; others criticized it.

In addition to writing books, Decter continued to contribute articles to periodicals during the 1980s, 1990s, and early 2000s.

SELECTED WORKS

The Liberated Woman and Other Americans (1970)
The New Chastity and Other Arguments against Women's Liberation (1972)
Liberal Parents, Radical Children (1975)
An Old Wife's Tale: My Seven Decades in Love and War (2001)

REFERENCES

Bernstein, Richard. "Neo-Con Culture Warrior Looks Back with Pride." *New York Times*, October 15, 2001, E7.
Decter, Midge. *An Old Wife's Tale: My Seven Decades in Love and War.* New York: Regan Books, 2001.
Gallagher, Dorothy. "No U-Turns." *New York Times*, September 16, 2001, BR20.

Daniel Defoe
(1660–1731)

DANIEL DEFOE, ACTUALLY DANIEL FOE, was born to Alice and James Foe in 1660. His father was a successful merchant and consequently was able to send Daniel to the best schools for Dissenters. Defoe attended Reverend James Fisher's school at Dorking, Surrey, England. Later, he attended Charles Morton's Academy in Newington Green, Middlesex, England.

Although Defoe studied for the Presbyterian ministry, he was attracted to business and subsequently became a merchant in Cornhill, London, England. He married Mary Tuffley, the daughter of a merchant, in 1684 and had several children. Defoe, for the most part, worked as a merchant in England and Scotland for the remainder of his life. However, he was not always successful. Indeed, by the early 1700s, he had been sued and had experienced bankruptcy.

Defoe actually wrote his first major pamphlet in 1688, which protested the policies of James II. He continued to write about politics using different forms, including satiric poems. For instance, in 1701, his poem "The True-Born Englishman," which defended William III, was immediately successful and catapulted him to national prominence. This success was short-lived, however. In 1702, he wrote *The Shortest Way with the Dissenters; or, Proposals for the Establishment of the Church*, which criticized Dr. Henry Sacheverell, a High Church priest, who did not notice the subtle humor. Sacheverell had Defoe imprisoned, for the church had political clout.

Robert Harley, the speaker of the House of Commons, knowing of Defoe's abilities as a writer, had him released in 1703. Harley realized that Defoe's talents could be used to shape public opinion; consequently, in 1704, he helped support *A Review of the Affairs of France, with Observations on Transactions at Home*, or the *Review*, a journal Defoe published intermittently until 1714. The journal served Harley's purposes on numerous issues.

England's political atmosphere was intense at the time. Indeed, it was hard to distinguish Tories from Whigs, and in reality each party controlled the House of Commons intermittently from 1679 to 1722. During this period, there were seventeen elections. Instability was rampant, so much so that in 1695, after years of not being enforced, the Licensing Act, which had been established to regulate printers and what was published, was a law of the past. As clashes between the king and Parliament increased, each realized the significance of printers in terms of their ability to shape public opinion. To license them, each believed, would be politically unsound. In addition, the rise of the two-party system made it difficult to enforce the act, since no particular person or party remained in power long enough to oversee its implementation. Consequently, since there was no effective prepublication censorship, "an explosion of polemical literature in the form of newspapers, newsletters, journals, pamphlets, broadsides, lampoons, and so forth" resulted.[1]

Defoe, of course, was one of the better writers, and the *Review* was one of the most popular publications. Laura Ann Curtis emphasized,

> He was an enthusiastic supporter of the Revolution of the hereditary Protestant monarchy it prescribed, of the fundamental rights of Parliament and people it recognized, not to be dispensed with by royal prerogative, and of the legal toleration it entailed for Protestant Dissenters. . . . He advocated . . . negotiations for the union of England and Scotland. An outspoken opponent of the theories of divine right and of passive obedience professed by adherents of the Stuart dynasty, a ridiculer of Jacobites (supporters of James II and of his son, the Pretender), Defoe contributed

to turning England away from its Stuart past to the present of its revolution settlement.[2]

However, it was his partisanship—his loyalty to Harley—that caused the decline in readers and ultimately the demise of the *Review*. When Harley ousted Godolphin and the Whigs in 1710, Defoe supported him; Defoe was considered by many to be a traitor. After having supported the war with France, he advocated peace; after having regarded France as England's economic rival, he advocated commercial trade. People did not know which side he favored because of his chameleon-like personality.

Defoe supported Harley well. More important, he served England well. He realized that progress would only be made if advocates such as he raised issues and then persuaded the masses as well as certain political figures to act appropriately on those issues. As an advocate, he had no rival. Unfortunately, he brought about his own fall by his own contrariness. Political propaganda replaced logic in his writing, and his credibility as a journalist suffered. As an advocate, however, his political conviction enabled him to present his point of view without having to contemplate the consequences. After all, any journalist who claims to be an advocate must have political convictions to present his or her side of an issue.

In addition to advocacy reporting, Defoe wrote realistic, fact-based stories such as *The Life and Strange Surprising Adventures of Robinson Crusoe, of York, Mariner*, which was published in 1719 and was inspired by Alexander Selkirk's unfortunate lengthy stay on the island of Juan Fernandez in 1704, and *The Fortunes and Misfortunes of the Famous Moll Flanders*, which was published in 1722 and described in intimate detail the lower orders of London society. However, his realistic stories merely introduced him to another form of writing—the nonfiction novel. Indeed, Defoe amplified his talent in the dramatic account *A Journal of the Plague Year: Being Observations or Memorials, of the Most Remarkable Occurrences, as Well Publick as Private, Which Happened in London during the Last Great Visitation in 1665, Written by a Citizen Who Continued All the While in London*, which was published in 1722 and accurately recorded the history of the Great Plague in London. Although Defoe had been five years old at the time of the Great Plague, he made use of what he remembered and what other survivors told him. Unquestionably fiction based on fact, the book was read by many who believed that the author had witnessed countless deaths; ironically, it was written more than fifty years after the disease ravaged England. Defoe based his book on contemporary accounts of the plague.

Defoe described the horror from the point of view of a citizen who recounted what he saw and heard. His style, simple and direct, added to "the awe-inspiring nature of the catastrophe."[3] The reader learned about certain characters, including their economic status and their personality.

Defoe practiced advocacy journalism as a result of the political and social turmoil that confronted England. He turned to the novel based on fact when his popularity as an advocate started to decline.

Defoe died in 1731.

SELECTED WORKS

"The True-Born Englishman" (1701)

The Shortest Way with the Dissenters; or, Proposals for the Establishment of the Church (1702)

A Review of the Affairs of France, with Observations on Transactions at Home (Review) (founder, 1704)

NOTES

1. Laura Ann Curtis, ed., The Versatile Defoe: An Anthology of Uncollected Writings by Daniel Defoe (Totowa, N.J.: Rowman & Littlefield, 1979), 4.

2. Curtis, The Versatile Defoe, 5–6.

3. George A. Aitken, ed., The Tatler (New York: Hadley & Mathews, 1899), ix.

REFERENCES

Backscheider, Paul R. *Daniel Defoe: His Life*. Baltimore, Md.: Johns Hopkins University Press, 1989.

Curtis, Laura Ann, ed. *The Versatile Defoe: An Anthology of Uncollected Writings by Daniel Defoe*. Totowa, N.J.: Rowman & Littlefield, 1979.

FitzGerald, Brian. *Daniel Defoe: A Study in Conflict*. Chicago: Regnery, 1955.

Novak, Maximillian E. *Daniel Defoe: Master of Fictions: His Life and Ideas*. Oxford: Oxford University Press, 2001.

Whitten, Wilfred. *Daniel Defoe*. New York: Haskell House, 1974.

Sarah Margaret Fuller (Marchesa D'Ossoli) (1810–1850)

BORN ON MAY 23, 1810, in Cambridgeport, Massachusetts, Sarah Margaret Fuller, later Marchesa D'Ossoli, was the eldest of nine children. Her mother, Margaret Crane Fuller, a teacher, and her father, Timothy Fuller, a lawyer and politician, provided their daughter with a vigorous education. Indeed, her father taught her to read Latin and English before she was six. She read works by Horace, Ovid, Virgil, Shakespeare, Henry Fielding, Tobias Smollett, Moliere, and Cervantes, among others. Fuller eventually learned Greek and other languages.

Fuller attended a school in Boston, which she enjoyed, and then Miss Prescott's School for Young Ladies in Groton, Massachusetts, which she did not enjoy. Most of her formal education, however, occurred at home. By the time she was sixteen, she was a brilliant conversationalist, and her friends included James Freeman Clarke, William Henry Channing, and later Frederick Henry Hedge, who introduced her to certain German writers as well as to philosophy.

Fuller studied and read most of the day. In addition to understanding several languages, she now understood mathematics, the Bible, and the works of Goethe, Madame de Stael, and George Sand.

In 1833, Fuller's father retired from public life and purchased a farm near Groton. He spent the next two years writing his memoirs but died unexpectedly in 1835. Fuller, who had been taking care of her younger brothers and sisters because her mother was ill, now was responsible for supporting the family.

In 1836, Fuller started teaching at Bronson Alcott's Temple School in Boston. Although the school was progressive, Fuller's salary was insufficient. To supplement her income, she taught several evenings a week in her Boston apartment and translated aloud various works for Dr. William Channing, whose eyesight was poor. The same year she met Ralph Waldo Emerson. She also began working on a biography of Goethe, which was never published, and translations for John Dwight's edition of *Select Minor Poems, Translated from the German of Goethe and Schiller*. She moved to Providence, Rhode Island, in 1837, where she taught at the Hiram Fuller's Greene Street School and received a higher salary. The same year she joined the Transcendentalism Symposium Club; she was the first woman to be accepted as a member. Members would meet and discuss various issues pertaining to philosophy or literature.

Fuller translated Johann Eckermann's *Conversations with Goethe in the Last Years of His Life* in 1839, the year she resigned from teaching at the Greene Street School. She moved to Boston and organized the famous "Conversations with Women," a series of meetings with educated women of the community. The first meeting's topic was Greek mythology. Fuller introduced the topic, presented a few ideas, then suggested a specific direction for the discussion. The meetings were so popular that she was asked to organize another series the following year. Eventually, men of prominence were invited to participate.

In 1840, Fuller was persuaded by Ralph Waldo Emerson to edit the *Dial: A Magazine for Literature, Philosophy, and Religion*, a journal that was about to be launched by the Transcendentalism Symposium Club. Fuller, who not only respected but admired Emerson, accepted. Unfortunately, members of the club believed in individuality, not teamwork, but a successful journal must have several supporters, if not staff members. Several prominent members, including her friend Frederick Henry Hedge, refused to write for the journal. To make matters worse, before the first issue was published, disagreement concerning the preface occurred between

Emerson and George Ripley. Eventually, however, the first issue was published. Dated July 1840, the journal contained 136 pages and included "The Divine Presence in Nature and the Soul" by Theodore Parker, "Short Essay on Critics" by Fuller, "The Religion of Beauty" by John Sullivan Dwight, "Orphic Sayings" by Bronson Alcott, and other work, including poetry.

By the end of the first year, the journal had few subscribers. Fuller, who had worked extremely hard to put out a journal that did not pay its contributors, had not been paid, either, even though she was supposed to earn an income as editor. The journal was sometimes criticized for its philosophy. Nonetheless, Fuller remained as editor of the journal for another year. Finally, Elizabeth Peabody, the new publisher, advised Fuller to relinquish her responsibilities because of her ill health. Fuller, who had been teaching, writing for other publications, and conducting "Conversations" to earn a living, left the *Dial* in March 1842. Emerson became the new editor. As Emerson and others admitted, however, had it not been for Fuller's sacrifices and tenacity, the journal would not have survived.

Fuller rested and visited relatives as well as Brook Farm, which had been started by George Ripley in 1841. Fuller believed that Ripley's experiment in communal living was worth trying, but she never joined. She was a frequent visitor, however.

In November 1842, Fuller conducted another series of "Conversations" in Boston, from which she earned enough to travel to the Midwest with friends. Like other writers of the period, Fuller kept a diary of her journeys, recording the places she visited as well as the individuals she met.

During this time, at the request of Emerson, Fuller contributed essays and reviews to the *Dial*. Her writing, which had concerned literature, painting, sculpture, and music, now concerned women. Her essay "The Great Lawsuit. Man *versus* Men. Woman *versus* Women" appeared as the lead article in the July 1843 issue and was the first major plea for women's rights in America to see print; it was read by both men and women around the world. Fuller became famous as a result of her advocating essay.

On her return from the Midwest, Fuller conducted another series of "Conversations" and started researching and writing *Summer on the Lakes, in 1843*, which concerned her experiences in the Midwest. She was the first woman to use the library at Harvard. *Summer on the Lakes, in 1843*, a travel book, contained an assortment of writing, including book reviews, translations, art criticism, short stories, and lengthy excerpts from other books. Fuller addressed various subjects—from the American Indians who inhabited the area to settlers who lived in peculiar surroundings. The book raised numerous questions about establishing a civilized society among so-called savages, and Fuller shared her insights and beliefs in an interesting mixture of writing styles.

The book was published in 1844. Fuller then expanded the essay "The Great Lawsuit. Man *versus* Men. Woman *versus* Women" into the book *Woman in the Nineteenth Century*. Fuller focused her attention on the social disadvantages experienced by women by relying on the lives of women in fiction rather than on real people. In her commentary about these characters, she identified the works that she considered the most valuable as well as the figures that provided positive role models for real women. Fuller attacked the hypocrisy of men and pleaded for equality for women. She disliked the stereotypical roles in which men and women had been cast. Through discussing characters such as Margaret in *Faust*, Fuller impressed on the female reader characters that had high moral principles. The book was published in 1845 and was without question her most important work.

Horace Greeley, the publisher of the *New York Daily Tribune*, offered Fuller a job as literary critic and social commentator. Greeley had been impressed by Fuller's ability to write. Accepting the offer, Fuller left New England for New York City in 1844. Emerson and transcendentalism were left behind. Instead of focusing on literary heroines and theories, she now focused on real life and became romantically involved with James Nathan. She produced at least two articles on literary subjects and at least one article on society every week. Fuller was also responsible for finding topics in the foreign press; these were discussed in editorials written by Greeley. She examined real women and sometimes the horrifying circumstances in which they found themselves—from serving time in prison to being committed to insane asylums. Fuller's observations reinforced her beliefs that society needed to be reformed.

Fuller's critical reviews were balanced, for the most part, in the sense that she presented the weaknesses as well as the strengths of a writer's work. She examined writers such as Elizabeth Barrett Browning, Ralph Waldo Emerson, Eugene Sue, Henry Wadsworth Longfellow, John Milton, Percy Bysshe Shelley, Caroline Kirkland, Lydia H. Sigourney, Henry R. Schoolcraft, Frederick Douglass, and Sylvester Judd.

In 1846, Fuller accompanied Marcus and Rebecca Spring to Europe, where she met prominent writers and politicians and observed the working-class poor. Fuller recorded the places and people she saw and met and later expanded her notes into articles for the *Daily Tribune*. The same year a collection of some of her essays was published. Titled *Papers on Literature and Art*, the essays concerned American and European literature and art.

Fuller met Thomas Carlyle, Thomas de Quincey, and William Wordsworth in Great Britain and George Sand in France. In 1847, she and the Springs traveled to Italy, where she visited several cities, finally settling in Rome. Fuller met Marchese Giovanni Angelo D'Ossoli, a member of a prominent Italian family. He was considerably younger than Fuller; nonetheless, he was attracted to her. When Fuller returned from a trip to northern Italy, they became romantically involved. Although it is not known whether they married before Angelo Eugene Philip was born in 1848, most biographers assume they married. Fuller kept her involvement with him secret, but his family learned of it and grew so angry that they disinherited him.

They became active participants in the Italian Revolution, which was a struggle for self-rule and independence. Fuller mailed dispatches to the *Daily Tribune*, and he served in the Civic Guard. Guiseppe Mazzini, an Italian patriot, gained control in 1849. The French attacked Rome, however, and eventually gained control several months later. Fuller, in addition to submitting dispatches to the *Daily Tribune*, served as "Regolatrice" of the government's military hospital, where she spent days comforting the wounded. When the French gained power, she obtained passports for Mazzini and other leaders of the revolution; then she and D'Ossoli fled Rome for Rieti and Florence.

By this time Fuller was using the name "D'Ossoli." When Horace Greeley learned of her questionable relationship that had produced a son, he stopped publishing her columns. Suddenly Fuller and D'Ossoli had no income. She had almost finished a manuscript on the history of the Italian Revolution, but it had not been shown to any publisher.

In 1850, Fuller borrowed money from friends so she and her family could sail to the United States. En route, the ship's captain died of smallpox. Fuller's son almost died from the same disease. When the ship was near the United States, a storm forced it off course, and it went aground off Fire Island and sank. Although some passengers and crew members were saved, Fuller, D'Ossoli, and their son were not. Some of Fuller's diaries and letters washed ashore, but her manuscript regarding the history of the Italian Revolution was lost.

Fuller was a major force behind the *Dial*. Indeed, she was responsible for the publication's modest success during its first two years. For this she will always have a place in American literature. Although most of her writing was not representative of advocacy journalism, *Woman in the Nineteenth Century* contained controversial ideas regarding women in society.

SELECTED WORK

Woman in the Nineteenth Century (1845)

REFERENCES

Blanchard, Paula. *Margaret Fuller: From Transcendentalism to Revolution*. New York: Delacorte, 1978.
Brown, Arthur W. *Margaret Fuller*. New York: Twayne, 1964.
Capper, Charles. *Margaret Fuller: An American Romantic Life*. 2 vols. New York: Oxford University Press, 1992–2007.
Chevigny, Bell Gale. *The Woman and the Myth: Margaret Fuller's Life and Writings*. Old Westbury, N.Y.: Feminist, 1976.
Stern, Madeleine B. *The Life of Margaret Fuller*. New York: Dutton, 1942.

Paul Goodman
(1911–1972)

PAUL GOODMAN WROTE SHORT STORIES, poetry, novels, essays, and books that advocated New Left ideology, even though he considered himself a conservative. He became popular among the radical youth of the 1960s as a result of his book *Growing Up Absurd*.

Born September 9, 1911, in Greenwich Village in New York City, Goodman was the youngest of three children. His father deserted the family when Goodman was an infant. His mother and older sister worked to support the family; his older brother left home when he reached maturity.

Goodman attended a Hebrew elementary school and Townsend Harris High School, from which he received his diploma in 1927. He attended the College of the City of New York for four years, earning his bachelor's degree in 1931.

Metro-Goldwyn-Mayer hired Goodman to read screenplays. At night, he attended classes at Columbia University, even though he had not registered for the courses. One paper he wrote for one of the classes was published in the *Journal of Philosophy* in 1934; it concerned neoclassicism, Platonism, and romanticism. He published several short stories in the annual *New Directions in Prose and Poetry* and several essays in the *Symposium*.

Goodman contributed criticism and poetry to the *Partisan Review* in the late 1930s and later contributed to other publications, including *Poetry* and the *Nation*.

Although Goodman began work toward a doctorate before 1940 at the University of Chicago, he was dismissed for homosexual activity.

Goodman published several poems and an essay in 1941 and the first novel in The Empire City series a year later. A book of short stories followed in 1945. *Art and Social Nature*, a collection of essays, and *The State of Nature*, the second novel in The Empire City series, were published in 1946. Although *Kafka's Prayer*, an analysis of Kafka's writings, was published in 1947, it was overshadowed by *Communitas: Means of Livelihood and Ways of Life*, which was cowritten with his older brother, Percival. This book attempted to inform the serious reader in words and illustrations how metropolitan areas could be developed or improved through careful planning.

The third novel in The Empire City series appeared in 1950. Titled *The Dead of Spring*, it was for the most part unnoticed by critics and readers. The same year another collection of short stories appeared.

Goodman worked as a lay psychologist with the New York Institute for Gestalt Therapy, and in 1951, with Dr. Frederick Perls and Ralph Hefferline, he wrote *Gestalt Therapy*. Another novel was published a year later. Goodman was recognized by critics and scholars when his doctoral dissertation, *The Structure of Literature*, was published by the University of Chicago Press in 1954. Goodman finally earned his doctorate the same year.

Goodman suffered from an inferiority complex. His sexual orientation and his unsteady income put a strain on his marriage, and he grew depressed. The fact that publishers were not interested in his writing did not help, either.

Although the novels of The Empire City were published as one work in 1959 and received favorable criticism, Goodman had not known financial success until his book *Growing Up Absurd: Problems of Youth in the Organized System* was published in 1960. Goodman, in this indictment against society, found society to be deficient in providing many of the most elementary opportunities and goals that could make growing up less difficult. The book appealed to thousands of young people who had grown disillusioned with the

American dream. As Taylor Stoehr wrote, "He pointed out how the wave of juvenile delinquency paralleled the beatnik subculture in the same urban centers, and he argued that both forms of rebellion were responses to the organized system, equally familiar territory mapped by everyone from George Orwell to Erich Fromm."[1]

According to Goodman, the young had a right to rebel. After all, if a society failed to provide them with meaningful work, sexual freedom, food for thought, and a community that they could be proud of, what purpose did it serve? Of course, the older generation dismissed Goodman, believing that he was naive about the world and perhaps life.

In 1962, a collection of Goodman's essays was published under the title *Drawing the Line*. One essay, "May Pamphlet," which he had written in 1945, explained why Goodman, a pacifist, disagreed with his draft board during World War II. There is little question that this essay encouraged hundreds of young people to dodge the draft in the mid- to late 1960s. The same year Goodman focused on the problems confronting higher education in *The Community of Scholars*, criticizing the inflated bureaucratic administrations for caring more about dollars than students.

In 1964, Goodman explored the exploited class—students— and presented possible alternatives to the traditional forms of education. In this work titled *Compulsory Mis-Education*, Goodman suggested that the traditional forms of education had failed.

Goodman published several collections of short stories, essays, and poetry in the 1960s as well, but most critics dismissed his fiction and poetry, claiming that both were too political and sociological in tone.

Before his death on August 2, 1972, Goodman had served as an editor at *Liberation*, a New Left publication, for twelve years and had written several books of literary criticism.

SELECTED WORKS

Growing Up Absurd: Problems of Youth in the Organized System (1960)

Drawing the Line (1962)
The Community of Scholars (1962)
Compulsory Mis-Education (1964)

NOTE

1. Taylor Stoehr, "Growing Up Absurd—Again: Rereading Paul Good-man in the Nineties," *Dissent* (Fall 1990), 487.

REFERENCES

Stoehr, Taylor. *Here Now Next: Paul Goodman and the Origins of Gestalt Therapy*. San Francisco: Jossey-Bass, 1994.
Widmer, Kingsley. *Paul Goodman*. Boston: Twayne, 1980.

Vivian Gornick (1935-)

VIVIAN GORNICK, A FEMINIST WHO TAUGHT English at the State University of New York at Stony Brook and later at Hunter College of the City University of New York, was born in New York City in 1935. She attended City College of the City University of New York, from which she received her bachelor's degree in 1957, and New York University, from which she received her master's degree in 1960.

Gornick, who wrote explicitly about women in contemporary society and the frustrations they endured from forced stereotyped sex roles, worked as a staff writer for the *Village Voice* from 1969 to 1977. Her investigative, advocating essays were collected and published in 1978 under the title *Essays in Feminism*. In the introduction, she explained that the collection seemed to be "a reflection of the manner in which American feminists—both as individuals and as a movement—have been coming of age in this past decade."[1] To Gornick, "The feminist perspective has grown measurably throughout American life because feminist consciousness has thrived and become ever more sophisticated whereas feminist dogma has shriveled and become ever more parochial."[2]

Gornick's essays, which explored such themes as liberation, lesbianism, feminist writers, the women's movement, Virginia Woolf, Dorothy Thompson, and Margaret Fuller, reminded the reader that few, if any, progressive steps had been made since her essays had first appeared in the *Village Voice*.

"On the Progress of Feminism: The Light of Liberation Can Be Blinding" was indicative of Gornick's straightforward style and her ability to advocate as well as inform. More personal, perhaps, than most of the advocacy reporting of the late 1960s and early 1970s, Gornick's piece revealed that she was extremely close to her subject. Although it would seem she would be in favor of feminists who revel in their verbal castration of men, Gornick's position was reserved, farsighted, and logical, for she looked ahead to the future. She realized that name-calling merely caused frustration, which ultimately drained the body—physically as well as mentally. Consequently, she encouraged her sisters to look ahead, to concentrate their efforts on tomorrow and on the end of the road. Although Gornick provided few, if any, facts to support her point, facts in this instance were not needed because her piece was spiritual in tone.

In 1983, after interviewing more than one hundred women scientists, Gornick's book *Women in Science: Portraits from a World in Transition* was published. She presented an impressionistic, journalistic portrait of women who worked in science and disclosed their diverse problems and ambitions related to their chosen careers.

Four years later, Gornick wrote *Fierce Attachments: A Memoir*, an autobiography that covered three years. She disclosed the struggle between her, a modern American woman, and her mother, an immigrant Jew. Needless to say, the bond between the two was complex. Gornick also examined other aspects of her life, including her relationships with men as well as her professional aspirations. Among the book's numerous literary devices, flashbacks depicted the characters at various stages in their lives.

In 1996, her book *Approaching Eye Level: Personal Essays* was published, providing valuable insight into how she thought. *The End of the Novel of Love: Critical Essays* followed a year later. Gornick examined romantic love in the lives and literary works of various writers, including Kate Chopin and Willa Cather. In 2001, her book *The Situation and the Story: The Art of Personal Narrative* was published.

In 2005 her book *The Solitude of Self: Thinking about Elizabeth Cady Stanton* was published, followed by *The Men in My Life* in 2008. The latter concerned various male writers and some of their work.

SELECTED WORKS

Essays in Feminism (1978)
Approaching Eye Level: Personal Essays (1996)

NOTES

1. Vivian Gornick, *Essays in Feminism* (New York: Harper & Row, 1978), 1.
2. Gornick, *Essays in Feminism*, 2.

REFERENCES

Gornick, Vivian. *Essays in Feminism*. New York: Harper & Row, 1978.
———. *Fierce Attachments: A Memoir*. New York: Simon & Schuster, 1987.

Meg Greenfield
(1930–1999)

MARY ELLEN GREENFIELD (she derived "Meg" from her initials) was born in Seattle, Washington, in 1930, to Lorraine and Lewis Greenfield, a successful antique furniture dealer. Her mother died before she was a teenager; her father became immersed in his business. Greenfield, a very good student, attended Smith College, from which she graduated summa cum laude in 1952. She received a Fulbright Scholarship and studied English literature at Cambridge University in England. Later, she lived briefly in Rome, Italy, before she moved to New York City.

Greenfield worked for Adlai Stevenson's presidential campaign in 1956. A year later she joined the staff of the *Reporter*, a liberal opinion magazine that focused on political issues. She worked as a researcher for several years. In 1960, she wrote "The Prose of Richard M. Nixon," a satiric profile of the presidential candidate. The article was widely discussed by readers and writers. Greenfield was promoted and became a correspondent in 1961; then she was promoted to editor of the Washington Bureau in 1965. She remained with the magazine until it ceased publication three years later.

Philip Geyelin, editor of the editorial page of the *Washington Post*, hired Greenfield as a writer. She was promoted to deputy editor of the editorial page in 1970 at the urging of Katharine Graham, the newspaper's publisher. Greenfield and Graham had become good friends. However, having a woman serve in this capacity was unusual for the time. Indeed, men, not women, filled such positions at most major metropolitan dailies.

In 1974, Greenfield started writing a biweekly column for *Newsweek*, which the Washington Post Company owned. The column, which brought her national recognition, focused on life in Washington and, of course, politics.

In 1978, Greenfield was awarded the Pulitzer Prize for commentary. The following year, when Geyelin stepped down as editorial page editor, she was promoted to the position. For the next twenty years, she was a stalwart figure at the *Post*. She supervised the editorial page staff, guiding it through one president's administration and its problems after another. She also contributed articles to the editorial pages over the years. She discovered several talented people, including George F. Will and Charles Krauthammer, among others, and encouraged them to consider journalism as a profession.

Greenfield enjoyed editorials that were based on fact; she did not care for editorials that were based merely on the writers' gut reactions to policies or issues. She was interested in learning about what actually occurred. She was not interested in someone's version or "spin" of it. She enjoyed writers who could discuss factually the military as well as political issues. She favored topics such as civil rights and nuclear strategy. Under her guidance, the editorial staff took mostly a liberal view toward social issues and a conservative view toward foreign policy and national defense. For instance, she and her staff opposed capital punishment but defended abortion rights. She and her staff opposed communism.

In addition to being responsible for the editorial page, Greenfield and her staff were responsible for the letters to the editor, the op-ed page, and two other pages that appeared in the weekend papers.

Although Greenfield was one of the first females to manage an editorial page staff, she was not necessarily an advocate for women's liberation, though she supported the feminists in some of their causes. However, she desired to be called "Miss—not Ms.—Greenfield" whenever she was addressed.

She was opposed to the editorial staff accepting material from public relations firms and incorporating it in articles that appeared in the newspaper. To her, this was unethical. Ethics was an important topic to her. Indeed, one of her early columns had concerned the hypocrisy of Spiro T. Agnew, President Nixon's vice president, who had spoken often about evildoers and wrongdoing. Yet, Agnew had to resign from office primarily because of a federal investigation into allegations of bribery and extortion. Apparently Agnew could not admit that he had been one of the evildoers about whom he had been speaking.

Greenfield also wrote about other politicians. For instance, she wrote about President Bill Clinton and his relationship with Monica Lewinsky, a White House intern, in relation to public versus private behavior as it related to the conduct of the nation's business. Greenfield believed that President Clinton needed to take responsibility for his actions.

She also wrote about her profession, especially whenever a mistake was made by a journalist or editor. After all, she reasoned, journalism as a profession was not above examination or criticism.

Greenfield lived in Georgetown, not far from Katharine Graham. Later, she had a house built on Bainbridge Island, near Seattle, where her brother's children lived. She died of cancer at her home in Georgetown; she was sixty-eight.

SELECTED WORKS

The *Reporter* (editor, Washington Bureau)
The *Washington Post* (editor, Editorial Page)

REFERENCES

Barringer, Felicity. "Meg Greenfield, Shaper of Washington Post Editorial Page and Public Policy, Dies at 68." *New York Times*, May 14, 1999, A25.
Greenfield, Meg. *Washington*. New York: Public Affairs, 2001.
Roberts, Chalmers McGeagh. *In the Shadow of Power: The Story of the Washington Post*. Revised and updated. Cabin John, Md.: Seven Locks Press, 1989.

Schaefer, Naomi. "Sisterhood Is Weak." *New Republic* 220, no. 23 (June 7, 1999): 15–16.

Smith, J. Y. "Post Editor, Newsweek Columnist Meg Greenfield Dies." *Washington Post*, May 14, 1999, A1.

Germaine Greer (1939–)

BORN IN AUSTRALIA TO ERIC AND MARGARET GREER on January 29, 1939, Germaine Greer was educated at the Star of the Sea Convent in Gardenvale, close to Melbourne. She left home at eighteen and enrolled at the University of Melbourne, where she received a bachelor's degree in 1959. She attended the University of Sydney, from which she obtained a master's degree two years later. Then she attended Newnham College, Cambridge, England, where she earned a doctorate in 1967.

Greer taught English at the University of Warwick and contributed a column to the *Sunday Times*, in London, for a few years. Before 1970, she cofounded the pornographic newspaper *Suck*. She also contributed articles to several publications such as *Oz*, the *Spectator*, the *Listener*, and *Esquire*.

She enjoyed the camaraderie of the musicians and actors of London, and she was somewhat of a celebrity before she wrote the best-selling feminist book *The Female Eunuch*. However, when the book was published in 1970, she was sought after by the media on both sides of the Atlantic. Her book—which argued that women had been stereotyped "Eternal Feminine" by society and men who, in actuality, had castrated women's sexuality through such characteristics as "timidity, plumpness, languor, delicacy and preciosity"—called for a revolution of spirit. As Greer put it:

Sex must be rescued from the traffic between powerful and pow-
erless, masterful and mastered, sexual and neutral, to become a
form of communication between potent, gentle, tender people,
which cannot be accomplished by denial of heterosexual contact.
The Ultra-feminine must refuse any longer to countenance the
self-deception of the Omnipotent Administrator, not so much by
assailing him as by freeing herself from the desire to fulfill his
expectations.[1]

Greer appeared on radio and television programs throughout
the United States and debated Norman Mailer. Although her spark
as a pronounced feminist was extinguished, her contribution to the
movement undeniably served a purpose.

Greer published *The Obstacle Race: The Fortunes of Women
Painters and Their Work* in 1979, in which she claimed that
there were no great female artists like Titian or Poussin because
women's egos had been damaged, their libidos had been driven
out of reach, and their energy had been diverted into neurotic
channels. The book, like her previous one, was an example of
advocacy journalism.

For several years Greer taught and later founded the Tulsa
Center for the Study of Women's Literature at the University of
Tulsa, in Oklahoma.

In 1984, she published *Sex and Destiny: The Politics of Human
Fertility*, an exhaustive inquiry into the Western world's attitudes
toward children, family, recreational sex, and the ways these con-
cepts had shaped policies around the world. Her discussion ranged
from childbirth, sterilization, and family planning to eugenics and
overpopulation. Greer claimed that the birthrate was falling in
Western societies because of a prevailing antichild attitude. She
approved of this attitude because the West consumed a dispropor-
tionate amount of natural resources. The book was criticized for its
seemingly antifeminist perspective.

Two years later she wrote the scholarly biography *Shakespeare*,
which discussed the playwright's life and work. This was followed
in 1987 by *The Madwoman's Underclothes: Essays and Occasional
Writings, 1968–1985*, which collected articles and essays that had
been published in newspapers and magazines. Greer examined

abortion, rape, pornography, and seduction, and each entry revealed her strengths and weaknesses both as a writer and as a woman in search of herself. Overall, the essays were about being white, middle-class, and extremely well educated, as well as about certain minorities, the poor, and the less educated.

In 1989, she wrote an insightful biography of her father. *Daddy, We Hardly Knew You* captured her father's life in Australia, as well as her search for who he really was. Greer also revealed how she confronted employees who worked in public offices for information about him.

Three years later, she focused on menopause. In *The Change: Women, Ageing, and the Menopause*, she showed how attitudes toward menopause had changed—or not—over time and urged women to question their ideas about the subject. The book seemed more personal than her other books on feminist issues.

In 1995, she wrote *Slip-Shod Sibyls: Recognition, Rejection and the Woman Poet*, in which she examined early as well as twentieth-century female poets, including Sappho, Elizabeth Barrett Browning, Sylvia Plath, and Anne Sexton, among others. Greer claimed that female poets were basically manipulated and to a certain extent intimidated by their male counterparts; as a result, they never achieved the status that their male counterparts achieved.

Four years later, she wrote *The Whole Woman*, in which she urged women to focus on liberation. She examined birth control, which she claimed was a ploy by males to keep women from having children, among other topics. Greer believed that culture had conditioned women to the point that they were not necessarily in control of their lives. Consequently, the purpose of her book was to point out this fact and to inform women about how they could break the chains that bound them.

Greer wrote *The Beautiful Boy* in 2003. Basically, she examined the age when a boy becomes a young man, which, she claimed, should be exciting to women, at least sexually speaking.

In 2007, she wrote *Shakespeare's Wife*, in which she examined the relationship between Shakespeare and his wife, Anne Hathaway. Although the book was based on research, many critics did not necessarily agree with the author's assertions.

SELECTED WORKS

The Female Eunuch (1970)
The Obstacle Race: The Fortunes of Women Painters and Their Work
　(1979)
Sex and Destiny: The Politics of Human Fertility (1984)
The Madwoman's Underclothes: Essays and Occasional Writings,
　1968–1985 (1987)
The Change: Women, Ageing, and the Menopause (1991)
The Whole Woman (1999)
The Beautiful Boy (2003)

NOTE

1. Germaine Greer, *The Female Eunuch* (New York: McGraw-Hill, 1971), 8.

REFERENCES

Britain, Ian. *Once an Australian.* Melbourne: Oxford University Press, 1998.

Greer, Germaine. *Daddy, We Hardly Knew You.* New York: Viking Penguin, 1989.

Plante, David. *Difficult Women: A Memoir of Three.* New York: Atheneum, 1983.

Ricketson, Matthew. *The Best Australian Profiles.* Melbourne: Black, 2004.

Wallace, Christine. *Germaine Greer: Untamed Shrew.* New York: Faber & Faber, 1997.

Pete Hamill (1935–)

BORN ON JUNE 24, 1935, to Anne and William Hamill in Brooklyn, New York, Pete Hamill said that he grew up in a state of rage. As he wrote in the introduction to his collection of *New York Post* columns, *Irrational Ravings*, "I had won a scholarship to a Jesuit high school called Regis. . . . Most of the students were upper-middle-class, and I spent the first few months there in a stage of desperate unhappiness."[1]

Hamill was reared in poverty and consequently learned early the ugliness of life, including injustice and bigotry. At sixteen, he dropped out of school to work in the Brooklyn Navy Yard, where he remained until he entered the navy. Hamill studied art and became familiar with the literature of Fitzgerald and Hemingway and was determined to return to school once he was discharged. He applied to Columbia University but was refused admittance. He tried to get a job as a copy boy at three New York City newspapers before he finally accepted a position as a messenger with an advertising agency. Eventually he moved to another agency and enrolled in advertising design courses at the Pratt Institute. Although advertising appealed to him at first, he grew bored with it by the time he reached twenty-five. In 1959, *Atlantis*, a Greek-language monthly magazine, published his first article. Hamill read the *New York Post* every day, especially Murray Kempton and Jimmy Cannon. Hamill wrote, "I didn't always understand Kempton, but there was something both elegant and passionate about his style that moved me and fed my angers. He had refined the great weapon of the fifties—irony—into something private and supple. But it was Cannon who made me want to be a newspaperman."[2]

In 1960, Hamill joined the *New York Post*, where he learned the fundamentals of journalism. Three years later, he became a contributing editor to the *Saturday Evening Post*, for which he traveled throughout Europe and wrote mostly about actors and actresses. He remained with the magazine until he was offered the chance to write a column for the *New York Post* two years later. Hamill said he would have become a minor league Damon Runyon if it had not been for Vietnam. He wrote, "The killings in Asia made it impossible to be Damon Runyon, and I started warring with myself in the column, torn between descriptive narratives and polemics."[3]

Hamill's column reflected what he sincerely believed about the war in Vietnam, the racial question, the differences between Brooklyn and Manhattan, the question of New York City being separated from New York, and the relationship between Arthur Goldberg, secretary of labor during John F. Kennedy's presidency, and U.S. policy in Vietnam, among other issues. If he decided to praise the Mets and criticize Mendel Rivers, chairman of the Armed Services Committee, even though Rivers was dead, readers eagerly read his views.

"Going Away," one of his columns, was indicative of his impressionistic style, which mixed narrative with dialogue. In simple, direct sentences, he not only realistically depicted scenes and characters but gave the reader homespun ideas to contemplate.

He resigned from the *Post* in 1967 when Bill Moyers, who had left the Johnson administration to become publisher of *Newsday*, asked him to become a Washington columnist. But when Hamill wrote a column attacking the president, an editor at *Newsday* prevented it from being published. Hamill resigned and completed his first novel, *A Killing for Christ*, which was published in 1968. Later, he contributed to the *Village Voice*, but when his friend Robert Kennedy was murdered, he suffered from writer's block. In 1969, he returned to the *New York Post* and also contributed articles to *New York, Ramparts, Playboy, Cosmopolitan, Life*, and

Esquire. Eventually he became a contributing editor to *New York* and *Esquire*.

In addition to articles, Hamill published several collections of short stories, including *Tokyo Sketches: Short Stories* in 1993, and novels, including *Flesh and Blood* in 1977, which concerned Bobby Fallon's rise as a professional boxer, and *Loving Women: A Novel of the Fifties* in 1988, which concerned an Irish kid from Brooklyn who journeyed through the South in the 1950s. He also wrote several screenplays and scripts for television, including "Report from Engine Co. 82" and "Death at an Early Age."

In 1994, he published his highly acclaimed autobiography, *A Drinking Life: A Memoir*, which affectionately told of the artist as a boy and as a young man and his thirst for alcohol. His father used to take him to bars. Pete was eight at the time. His mother never drank. She encouraged him to draw cartoons, which he enjoyed. Hamill recalled his life at eight, at sixteen, and at other ages. He wrote about life in Greenwich Village in the early 1950s. He explained that he joined the navy to see the world; however, he saw the bottom of numerous liquor bottles instead. He recalled his life as an art student in Mexico and as an apprentice reporter for the *New York Post*. He described his nights on the town. He claimed that his marriage deteriorated as a result of his addiction to alcohol. In 1972, Hamill examined his life and realized that he had to change. He put the bottle down on the counter and never picked it up again. The memoir was well written and proved that Hamill had the skill of a journalist and the insight of a novelist.

Another collection of columns was published in 1996; it was titled *Piecework: Writings on Men and Women, Fools and Heroes, Lost Cities, Vanished Friends, Small Pleasures, Large Calamities, and How the Weather Was.*

Two years later he published *News Is a Verb: Journalism at the End of the Twentieth Century.* The book, an insightful, critical examination of modern journalism, appeared after he had briefly served as editor of the *New York Daily News*.

Over the next several years, Hamill wrote several novels, including *Forever*, which was published in 2002, and *North River*, which was published in 2007. He also wrote nonfiction, including

Why Sinatra Matters, which was published in 1998, and *Downtown: My Manhattan*, which was published in 2004.

SELECTED WORKS

Irrational Ravings (1971)
A Drinking Life: A Memoir (1994)
Piecework: Writings on Men and Women, Fools and Heroes, Lost Cities, Vanished Friends, Small Pleasures, Large Calamities, and How the Weather Was (1996)
News Is a Verb: Journalism at the End of the Twentieth Century (1998)

NOTES

1. Pete Hamill, *Irrational Ravings* (New York: Putnam's, 1971), 15–16.
2. Hamill, *Irrational Ravings*, 25.
3. Hamill, *Irrational Ravings*, 27.

REFERENCES

Hamill, Pete. *Irrational Ravings*. New York: Putnam's, 1971.
———. *A Drinking Life: A Memoir*. Boston: Little, Brown, 1994.
———. *Downtown: My Manhattan*. Boston: Little, Brown, 2004.

Michael Harrington
(1928–1989)

MICHAEL HARRINGTON WAS BORN to Catherine and Edward Harrington, an attorney, on February 24, 1928, in St. Louis. After attending parochial schools, he enrolled in a Jesuit institution, Holy Cross College, in Worcester, Massachusetts. He received his bachelor's degree in 1947 and then entered Yale University Law School. Within a year, however, he was dissatisfied with law and with Yale University; he transferred to the University of Chicago, where he studied English literature. In 1949, he received his master's degree and returned to St. Louis, where he worked as a welfare worker until 1951.

Although Harrington was convinced that socialism was necessary to improve American society, he did not promote the idea until he moved to New York City, where he worked not only as a staff member of St. Joseph's House of Hospitality, which catered to derelicts, but also as an associate editor of the *Catholic Worker*. When he left the monthly publication in 1952, he joined the Workers Defense League. Then he became a researcher for the Fund for the Republic. For most of the 1950s, he gathered information and wrote various Fund projects, including at least one report on blacklisting in the entertainment industry.

Harrington, who enjoyed stimulating conversation with other socialists in Greenwich Village, contributed articles to such periodicals as the *Nation*, *Commentary*, the *New Republic*, *Commonweal*, the *Reporter, Harper's, Atlantic, Dissent,* and the *Village Voice.* From 1961 to 1962, Harrington edited *New America.* Throughout the 1960s, he was also associated with several socialist organizations, including the International Union of Socialist Youth, the League for Industrial Democracy, and the American Socialist Party.

In 1962, Harrington wrote the best-selling book *The Other America: Poverty in the United States,* in which he exposed the fact that while America was beginning to call itself the affluent society, some forty to fifty million Americans were poor both physically and spiritually. To say the least, the book was an indictment of the so-called American dream. Harrington called for immediate action because he realized that only the larger society could implement socialized programs that would alleviate some of the problems. The book was respectfully received by critics, and President John F. Kennedy, who read it, requested congressional action.

The Accidental Century, which defended democratic socialism and severely attacked capitalism, appeared in 1965. In *Toward a Democratic Left: A Radical Program for a New Majority,* which was published in 1968, Harrington exposed and analyzed the problems of American society, including the technological innovations of the Western world, which he believed created additional problems rather than remedies for man. He failed, however, to provide an overall plan that would correct the problems he discussed.

In 1973, Harrington formed the Democratic Socialist Organizing Committee. The goal was to forge a coalition of environmentalists, feminists, peace activists, racial and ethnic minorities who belonged to the Democratic Party, and trade unionists. The membership grew from two hundred members in 1973 to four thousand by 1980. In 1981 the Committee merged with the New American Movement to create the Democratic Socialists of America.

Harrington, who became editor of the newsletter *Democratic Left* in 1973, wrote additional books about America's problems and socialistic remedies throughout the 1970s and 1980s. For instance, he wrote two highly acclaimed books on political strategy in 1972 and 1976, respectively: *Socialism* and *The Twilight of Capitalism.* In 1977 and 1984, respectively, he returned to the subjects of poverty in *The Vast Majority: A Journey to the World's Poor* and *The New*

American Poverty. The last book discussed the structures that kept the underprivileged poor. According to Harrington, conservatism was the culprit, while socialism was the answer. The book was nominated for a National Book Award.

In 1980 and 1987, respectively, Harrington examined political issues in *Decade of Decision: The Crisis of the American System* and *The Next Left: The History of a Future*, which discussed how the nature of economic growth had changed. Investments, he claimed, could not create more jobs, but investments could create more national products. In three lengthy chapters, Harrington explained how the United States had progressed. He also explained how well-meaning social policies had actually harmed society.

In *The Next America: The Decline and Rise of the United States* and *The Politics at God's Funeral: The Spiritual Crisis of Western Civilization*, which were published in 1981 and 1983, respectively, Harrington described the cultural and spiritual crisis in American values and presented various versions of the country's future. He called for a public policy that would not only address American values but preserve them as well.

Harrington wrote two autobiographies—*Fragments of the Century: A Social Autobiography*, which was published in 1973 and which explored his life as well as his reasons for being a socialist, and *The Long-Distance Runner: An Autobiography*, which was published in 1988 and which included the account of how he brought about the merger of the two major socialist organizations in America in 1981. He also collected some of the essays and articles that he had written between 1955 and 1983 for the book *Taking Sides: The Education of a Militant Mind*, which was published in 1986. The essays covered various topics, including the politics of the peace movement, the political novel, and Disney World.

Harrington's last book, which was completed before he died of cancer on July 31, 1989, was titled *Socialism Past and Future* and was published in 1989. He called for reform such as state intervention in the retraining of the workforce and improving public education. He also requested that markets be pragmatically regulated and that leveraged buyouts be restrained.

In *The Accidental Century*, Harrington used simple words in simple sentences to make certain complex points comprehensible. Like other advocacy journalists, Harrington made his point and then supported it with facts. In one section, he argued that although corporations were no longer owned by any one person, the same outdated philosophy underlined their purpose. To Harrington, this philosophy was not necessarily good for the corporation, its employees, or society, and he supported his thesis with substantial evidence.

SELECTED WORKS

New America (editor)
Democratic Left (editor)
The Other America: Poverty in the United States (1962)
The Accidental Century (1965)
Toward a Democratic Left: A Radical Program for a New Majority (1968)
The Vast Majority: A Journey to the World's Poor (1977)
Decade of Decision: The Crisis of the American System (1980)
The Next America: The Decline and Rise of the United States (1981)
The Politics at God's Funeral: The Spiritual Crisis of Western Civilization (1983)
The New American Poverty (1984)
Taking Sides: The Education of a Militant Mind (1986)
The Next Left: The History of a Future (1987)

REFERENCES

Gorman, Robert A. *Michael Harrington—Speaking American.* New York: Routledge, 1995.
Harrington, Michael. *Taking Sides: The Education of a Militant Mind.* New York: Holt, 1985.

————. *The Long-Distance Runner: An Autobiography.* New York: Holt, 1988.

Isserman, Maurice. *The Other American: The Life of Michael Harrington.* New York: Public Affairs, 2000.

Nat(han) Hentoff
(1925–)

NAT HENTOFF WAS BORN to Lena and Simon Hentoff on June 10, 1925, in Boston, and was educated at the Boston Latin School, Northeastern University, from which he received his bachelor's degree in 1946, Harvard University, and the Sorbonne in Paris, France. From 1944 to 1953, he worked as an announcer, writer, and producer for a radio station in Boston. In 1953, he became an associate editor of *Downbeat* magazine. He also wrote musical reviews for *Hi Fi/Stereo Review*, the *New York Herald Tribune*, *Book Week*, the *Reporter*, and London's *Peace News*. In 1957, he became a columnist for the *Village Voice*, where his interest in jazz was replaced by an interest in sociological and political issues. An advocate, Hentoff wrote vehemently about such topics as civil rights, poverty, the draft, education, and police corruption.

In 1960, in addition to working for the *Village Voice* and contributing to such publications as *Inquiry* and *Liberation*, for which he once served as an associate editor, Hentoff became a staff writer for the *New Yorker*, where his interests grew more diverse. Several years later he also became a regular contributor to the *Progressive*.

Although Hentoff wrote several books about jazz, his advocacy journalism appeared in such books as *The New Equality*, which was published in 1964; *Our Children Are Dying*, which was published in 1966; and *Does Anybody Give a Damn? Nat Hentoff on Education*, which was published in 1977. In *The New Equality*, he criticized whites who, because of their guilt over the plight of African Americans, tried to guarantee civil rights reform. Such guarantees were preposterous to Hentoff, and he supported his thesis with credible evidence. In *Our Children Are Dying* and *Does Anybody Give a Damn?* which were written more than ten years apart, he explored the problems of the inner-city schools and provided several possible solutions. In the former, for instance, he introduced Elliott Shapiro, a principal in Harlem who faced numerous problems every day—from a deteriorated school building to a public school system that discouraged change. Yet Shapiro had numerous ideas that, if implemented, could have helped countless students pass their courses and subsequently graduate. In the latter book, Hentoff examined the public school system again and learned that little had been done to address the problems he discussed some ten years earlier.

Hentoff wrote *The First Freedom: The Tumultuous History of Free Speech in America* in 1980, which was inspired by his leaving the college paper staff at Northeastern University. As editor, he had been instrumental in having his staff write about anti-Semitism in Boston and question the administration of the university. In fact, Hentoff mentioned the authorities on the acknowledgments page of the book: "For my abiding concern with the First Amendment, I am particularly indebted to those officials at Northeastern University in Boston who tried to censor the writings of the staff when I was editor of the *Northeastern News* in the early 1940s. . . . I never lost my sense of rage at those who would suppress speech, especially mine. Those administrators truly helped inspire this book."[1]

In his book, Hentoff examined censorship in American society—from a libel case in 1735 to books being burned in 1973. He explored the subject of banning books in public and school libraries as well as the reasons for such actions, including obscenity. He discussed the Supreme Court's decisions and highlighted excerpts from the Court's printed opinions. The book's overall purpose was to inform the reader that most people involved in burning or banning books were not necessarily members of groups or members of Congress but were average citizens who questioned something they saw in print.

In 1986, Hentoff captured in a captivating autobiography the conflict between a first-generation orthodox Jewish youth and the varied ethnic communities that divided a city. Titled *Boston Boy*, the memoir covered his early years of growing up in an anti-Semitic Irish Catholic neighborhood. The book also chronicled Hentoff's emerging appreciation of jazz.

Hentoff wrote about John Cardinal O'Connor of New York City for the *New Yorker*. Then he wrote about him in the appropriately titled *John Cardinal O'Connor: At the Storm Center of a Changing American Church*, which was published in 1988. The biography detailed the life of the tough-minded defender of Pope John Paul II as well as the changing American Catholic Church.

In 1992, Hentoff wrote about free speech in *Free Speech for Me but Not for Thee: How the American Left and Right Relentlessly Censor Each Other*. He presented numerous case studies to illustrate the ongoing struggle between the advocates of civil rights and the advocates of civil liberties. Hentoff claimed that the threat to free speech came from the left, not from the right.

Hentoff wrote *Speaking Freely: A Memoir* in 1997. A year later he wrote *Living the Bill of Rights: How to Be an Authentic American*. In 2001, he published *The Nat Hentoff Reader*. He published *The War on the Bill of Rights—and the Gathering Resistance* in 2003.

Hentoff wrote columns for the *Washington Post* and the *Washington Times*; books for young people, including the popular *Jazz Country*, which was published in 1965; and several novels for adults, such as *The Man from Internal Affairs*, which was published in 1985 and which was a mystery that featured Lieutenant Noah Green of the New York Police Department.

SELECTED WORKS

The New Equality (1964)
Our Children Are Dying (1966)
Does Anybody Give a Damn? Nat Hentoff on Education (1977)
The First Freedom: The Tumultuous History of Free Speech in America (1980)

*Free Speech for Me but Not for Thee: How the American Left and
  Right Relentlessly Censor Each Other* (1992)
The Nat Hentoff Reader (2001)

NOTE

1. Nat Hentoff, *The First Freedom: The Tumultuous History of Free
Speech in America* (New York: Delacorte, 1980), 2.

REFERENCES

Foster, Harold M. "Nat Hentoff." *Writers for Young Adults*. Vol. 3. New
  York: Scribner's, 1997.
Hentoff, Nat. *Boston Boy*. New York: Knopf, 1986.
———. *Speaking Freely: A Memoir*. New York: Knopf, 1997.

Jill Johnston (1929–)

JILL JOHNSTON WAS BORN TO Olive Johnston and Cyril Frederick on May 17, 1929, in London, England. Her mother was an American, while her father was an English aristocrat who rejected his daughter as well as her mother. As a result, Johnston grew up thinking that she was more like an orphan than a child who had parents.

Johnston attended several universities, including the University of North Carolina at Greensboro, in the late 1940s and early 1950s. She married Richard Lanham in 1958 and had two children. However, she realized that a heterosexual lifestyle was not for her. Indeed, it was because of this realization that she was able to write so convincingly about the women's movement and lesbianism for the *Village Voice*, which she joined in 1959. Johnston started writing "Dance Journal," an artistic and critical column about avant-garde dance. Later, she explored herself and other feminists in articles. What and how she wrote reflected her opinions and attitudes. Occasionally, she became personally involved in what she wrote, almost to the point that her own and the subject's belief systems were one and the same.

She and Lanham divorced in 1964.

In 1971, she published a compilation of her columns under the title *Marmalade Me*. A year later she wrote about the women's movement in "The March of the Real Women." This and other articles focused on the divisions within the women's movement,

especially between straight people and lesbians. Johnston advocated having lesbians lead the women's movement because they
were not as confused sexually as straights.

In 1973, this idea and others were further explored in *Lesbian
Nation: The Feminist Solution*, a book about lesbianism as well as
feminism. Johnston then turned inward and examined herself in relation to others in articles and, later, a book. Her *Gullibles Travels* was
favorably reviewed by Susan Braudy in *Ms.*: "This overly sensitive,
unsettling, disruptive wonderwoman, this 'recalcitrant daughter' in
'high-denim dyke gear,' is one of our most original open-to-the-gut
feminist writers."[1] The essays in this book focused on women such
as Agnes Martin and Bella Abzug. In addition, Johnston depicted
herself, almost lifelike and on canvas, as she employed one persona,
then another. This book, perhaps more than any other, exhibited her
creative ability. In addition to using lowercase letters, particularly
when she referred to herself, she played with language.

In 1983, she wrote the first volume of her *Autobiography in
Search of a Father, Mother Bound*. In it Johnston explored herself
and her relationship with her parents. Two years later she wrote the
second volume, *Paper Daughter*, in which she continued her soul-
searching and obsession with her parents. As in the first volume,
she explored her life during the 1960s. She recounted her emo-
tional breakdowns, her lesbianism, and her newly acquired fame.
Both volumes were written in the same stream-of-consciousness
literary style used in *Gullibles Travels*.

Also, in the 1980s, she wrote for *Art in America*.

In 1994, she published *Secret Lives in Art: Essays on Art, Literature, Performance*. *Jasper Johns: Privileged Information*, a biography,
was published two years later. This was followed by *Admission Accomplished: The Lesbian Nation Years, 1970–75* in 1998. Ten years
later, she published *England's Child: The Carillon and the Casting
of Big Bells*.

SELECTED WORKS

Marmalade Me (1971)
Lesbian Nation: The Feminist Solution (1973)

Gullibles Travels (1974)
Secret Lives in Art: Essays on Art, Literature, Performance (1994)

NOTE

1. Susan Braudy, "The Johnston Papers," *Ms.*, October 1974, 36.

REFERENCES

Johnston, Jill. *Autobiography in Search of a Father: Mother Bound*. New York: Knopf, 1983.
———. *Autobiography in Search of a Father: Paper Daughter*. New York: Knopf, 1985.
Larkin, Joan. *A Woman Like That: Lesbian and Bisexual Writers Tell Their Coming Out Stories*. New York: Avon Books, 1999.

Matthew Josephson
(1899–1978)

MATTHEW JOSEPHSON WAS BORN IN Brooklyn in 1899 and attended Columbia University, from which he graduated in 1920. Attracted to European literature, especially the psychological literature of the French Symbolists, he traveled to Paris in 1921. He was drawn to the Dadaists primarily because they were carefree and unpredictable. Josephson appreciated their interest in literature; however, he realized they did not hold to literary conventions.[1]

Josephson tried to persuade his American friends Kenneth Burke, Malcolm Cowley, and Hart Crane to follow him to Paris. Unlike other writers he had met while living in Greenwich Village during the Bohemian period, he changed his philosophy and form of writing when neither was in vogue. For instance, when he realized that Americanization of France was approved and actually encouraged by the Dadaists, his philosophy changed accordingly. According to David E. Shi, "In Paris Josephson began promoting an artistic attitude that would accept the reality of modern life and use the machine and the modern idiom to aesthetic advantage."[2]

In 1922, Josephson and Gorham Munson founded *Secession*, a review that promoted his ideas and published such writers as Kenneth Burke, Louis Aragon, Philippe Soupault, Andre Briton, Malcolm Cowley, and Marianne Moore. His ideas, although controversial, were accepted in Europe but criticized in the United States. That same year, Josephson became an associate editor of

Broom, another literary magazine, and for the next two years, until the magazine's demise, he criticized American writers for not taking the initiative to experiment. Perhaps if Josephson had not returned to New York City in 1923 to start an American edition of *Broom,* the parent magazine would not have failed. Nonetheless, among the avant-garde magazines *Broom* had no equal.

After a brief stint on Wall Street, Josephson returned to writing in 1926; once again his philosophy changed. This time he attacked the Dadaists for their refusal to write about societal ills. A year later Josephson returned to France to gather information on Emile Zola. The biography that resulted was well received, and he immediately realized his potential in this genre.

In 1928, he became a contributing editor to *transition,* a magazine similar to *Broom,* except that its editors Elliot Paul and Eugene Jolas promoted Surrealism. His association with the magazine lasted for more than a year until he became so immersed in social and political issues that art and literature were no longer important. He was also gathering information for a biography of Jean-Jacques Rousseau, which was ultimately published in 1931.

During 1931 and 1932, Josephson worked as an assistant editor of the *New Republic,* a left-wing magazine, and supported the efforts of the Communist Party. His book *The Robber Barons: The Great American Capitalists, 1861–1901* examined the careers of such millionaires as Jay Gould, John D. Rockefeller, Henry Clay Frick, J. P. Morgan, Andrew Carnegie, and E. H. Harriman. Josephson noted, "They were aggressive men, as were the first feudal barons; sometimes they were lawless; in important crises, nearly all of them tended to act without those established moral principles which fixed more or less the conduct of the common people of the community. . . . These men were robber barons as were their medieval counterparts, the dominating figures of an aggressive economic age."[3]

Josephson's study was both factual and informative; every question raised was clearly answered. His book *The Politicos, 1865–1896,* which was similarly researched and written, appeared four years later.

For the next three decades, Josephson wrote biographies, political and social histories, and several volumes devoted to his life. He also contributed articles to the *Saturday Evening Post*, the *Nation*, *Outlook*, and the *New Yorker*.

Josephson died in 1978.

SELECTED WORKS

Secession (cofounder)
Broom (associate editor)
The Robber Barons: The Great American Capitalists, 1861–1901 (1934)
The Politicos, 1865–1896 (1938)

NOTES

1. David E. Shi, "Matthew Josephson," *American Writers in Paris, 1920–1939*, vol. 4, ed. Karen Lane Rood (Detroit: Gale Research, 1980), 232.

2. Shi, "Matthew Josephson," 233.

3. Matthew Josephson, *The Robber Barons: The Great American Capitalists, 1861–1901* (New York: Harcourt, Brace, 1934), vii.

REFERENCE

Shi, David E. *Matthew Josephson, Bourgeois Bohemian*. New Haven, Conn.: Yale University Press, 1981.

Murray Kempton
(1918-1997)

MURRAY KEMPTON WAS BORN ON December 16, 1918, in Baltimore to Sally and James Kempton, a stockbroker who died a few years after his son was born. Kempton attended public schools and Johns Hopkins University. Interested in history and political science, he became a member of the Socialist Party.

After he received his degree in 1939, he found employment as a social worker in Baltimore, where he remained for a few months. Then he moved to New York City, where he worked as an organizer for the American Youth Congress, specifically the Campaign for Youth Needs. Then he worked as an organizer for the International Ladies' Garment Workers' Union in Peekskill, New York. Experience at these positions enabled him to become publicity director for the American Labor Party and a writer for both the Young People's Socialist League and the Workers' Defense League in 1941.

A year later, Kempton was hired by the *New York Post* to report on labor, but his assignment was abruptly interrupted when he enlisted in the U.S. Army. For the remainder of World War II, he was engaged in combat in the Pacific. He returned to the United States unharmed.

For the next several years, he worked as a reporter for the Wilmington, North Carolina, *Star,* then as assistant to Victor Riesel, the labor editor of the *New York Post*. In 1949, he became the paper's labor editor and focused his attention on the relationships between union officials and members of organized crime. As a columnist, he covered civil rights and politics, including domestic and foreign policy as well as presidential campaigns. He was deeply concerned with the Red Scare created by Senator Joseph McCarthy, which he denounced. His attitude toward Communists was not necessarily favorable, but he believed that members of the Communist Party had rights. His book, *Part of Our Time: Some Ruins and Monuments of the Thirties*, explored this attitude and belief in depth.

During the 1950s, Kempton covered with equal candor the problems confronting African Americans. He addressed the problem of segregation, a practice he deemed unjust. He covered Autherine Juanita Lucy's first day at the University of Alabama as well as the controversial trial of two white men who were charged with the murder of an African American youth. These dispatches were so elegant in style that they were almost short stories.

Toward the end of the decade, he covered Nikita Khrushchev's tour of the United States. He also covered the 1960 presidential campaign. A year later he traveled to the South again and wrote about Dr. Martin Luther King Jr.'s desegregation campaign. The same year he defended Carmine DeSapio, New York's Tammany Hall leader. Kempton, who strongly believed in human rights, was severely criticized not only for having supported DeSapio but for having defended another columnist, Westbrook Pegler, who had been dismissed from the Hearst empire in 1962 for his right-wing philosophy.

A year later, Kempton left the *Post* and moved to Washington, D.C., where he worked as an editor and columnist for the *New Republic*. Kempton, who worked for over a year for the liberal weekly, wrote numerous articles about controversial issues and persons, including the "Warren Report," Jack Ruby, John F. Kennedy and his administration, and Joe Valachi. His second book, *America Comes of Middle Age: Columns 1950–1962*, which was published in 1963, was a collection of columns that had appeared in the *New York Post*.

From 1964 to 1966, he wrote columns for the *New York World Telegram and Sun*. He returned to the *Post* shortly thereafter and contributed a column through most of the 1970s. In addition, he contributed to numerous magazines and wrote *The Briar Patch: The People of the State of New York Versus Lumumba Shakur, et al.* in 1973. Kempton explored the deplorable injustice with which the U.S. court system treated the Black Panthers.

Although he threatened to leave the *Post* more than once throughout the 1970s, he remained with the paper until 1981, when he left to join *Newsday*, where his column appeared at least four times a week. In addition, he contributed essays to various publications throughout the 1980s and early 1990s. Some of these publications included *House and Garden*, the *Saturday Evening Post*, and the *New York Review of Books*. Kempton became a member of the editorial advisory board of the *Washington Monthly* during this time.

Kempton met numerous prominent people as well as members of organized crime during his more than fifty years in journalism, from Adlai Stevenson, Alger Hiss, Richard Nixon, Daniel Patrick Moynihan, Nancy Reagan, George Bush, and Ross Perot to Malcolm X, Martin Luther King Jr., Louis Armstrong, Huey Newton, Frank Costello, Carmine Persico, Jimmy Hoffa, John Gotti, Jean Harris, and William F. Buckley.

Rebellions, Perversities, and Main Events, which contained his columns and stories from the *Post* and *Newsday*, as well as lengthy essays from the *New York Review of Books*, was published in 1994. Together, the columns and essays exhibited Kempton's affection for the radical, the rebel, the rascal, the misfit, and the loser. Indeed, he complimented Alger Hiss for being a good comrade at Lewisburg Prison; he praised Lillian Hellman for her defiance of the House Committee on Un-American Activities. He examined with sarcastic criticism several presidents, including Truman, Eisenhower, and Nixon, who was a friend. Kempton also discussed Italy, Italians, and certain members of the Mafia, as well as jazz and art. Like most of his work, this collection revealed his ability to advocate worthy causes, defend the accused, and criticize individuals for unprofessional or unethical conduct, all in a literary and elegant style.

Kempton, who had been married twice and who had several children, developed pancreatic cancer. He died on May 5, 1997, in a nursing home in New York City.

SELECTED WORKS

Part of Our Time: Some Ruins and Monuments of the Thirties
   (1955)
America Comes of Middle Age: Columns 1950–1962 (1963)
Rebellions, Perversities, and Main Events (1994)

REFERENCES

Duggan, Dennis. "A Singular Spirit: Murray Kempton: A Legend of New
   York Journalism." *The Quill*, September 2004, 49.
Kempton, Murray. *Rebellions, Perversities, and Main Events*. New York:
   Times Books, 1994.
Remnick, David. "Prince of the City." *The New Yorker*, March 1, 1993:
   41–44, 46–54.
Severo, Richard. "Murray Kempton, 79, a Newspaperman of Honor and
   Elegant Vinegar, Is Dead." *New York Times*, May 6, 1997, A1.
Ward, Geoffrey C. "Unpackaged Goods." *American Heritage* 45, no. 5
   (September 1994): 10, 12.

Seymour Krim
(1922–1989)

BORN ON MAY 11, 1922, to Ida and Abraham Krim in New York City, Seymour Krim attended the University of North Carolina at Chapel Hill for a year and then returned home, where he obtained employment as a reporter for the *New Yorker*. Later, he wrote publicity features for Paramount Pictures, then became a story editor for Otto Preminger Productions.

Throughout the 1940s, he earnestly desired to write the great American novel, but he realized that in the midst of intellectual giants such as Ernest Hemingway, his talent as a writer could never propel him to such a height. Consequently, he became a book reviewer for the *New York Times Book Review* in 1947.

This experience enabled him to move to the *Commonweal*, where he was given the opportunity to write longer, in-depth pieces. *Commentary* and the *Partisan Review* opened their pages to him. Although he did not care for writing reviews, he produced one after another until he was offered a position with the *Hudson Review*, a periodical respected by readers for its depth and quality.

Krim's experience broadened. He became an essayist of unusual merit, and a critic whose writing was published in such periodicals as the *Village Voice*.

From 1961 to 1965, Krim was the editorial director of *Nugget*, a men's magazine, and from 1965 to 1966, he was a reporter for the *New York Herald Tribune*. He taught at several universities, including the University of Iowa, Pennsylvania State University, and Columbia University. Collections of his essays appeared under the titles *Views of a Nearsighted Cannoneer*, *Shake It for the World*, *Smartass*, and *You and Me*.

"Revolt of the Homosexual," which Krim wrote in 1958, was quite distinct from most essays. Instead of employing the traditional form to explain his position toward the subject, he used what could be described as either an interview or a conversation between a heterosexual and a homosexual. By using this approach, he made his point strongly.

Krim died of an apparent suicide in 1989. *What's This Cat's Story? The Best of Seymour Krim* was published in 1991.

SELECTED WORKS

Views of a Nearsighted Cannoneer (1961)
Shake It for the World, Smartass (1970)
You and Me (1974)

REFERENCES

Nicosia, Gerald. "Seymour Krim: Making Every Word Count." *Washington Post*, October 29, 1989, L1, 10.
"Seymour Krim: Author and Critic." *Washington Post*, September 3, 1989, D12.
Wenke, Joseph. "Seymour Krim." *The Beats: Literary Bohemians in Postwar America. Dictionary of Literary Biography*, Vol. 16. Ed. Ann Charters. Detroit: Gale Research, 1983.

Jeremy Larner (1937–)

NOVELIST AND SOCIAL REPORTER Jeremy Larner was born on March 20, 1937, to Clara and Martin Larner in Olean, New York. He received his bachelor's degree in 1958 from Brandeis University. He studied at the University of California at Berkeley until 1959. Although he wrote short stories and a few novels, including the satirical social farce *Drive, He Said*, which was published in 1964 and ultimately made into a movie in 1970, his stories and novels had less effect on readers than his factual articles on education in Harlem and poverty, which appeared in *Dissent*. These articles not only informed readers of the problems but inspired other writers to investigate the conditions and produce further findings. Some, like Larner, advocated that the problems be corrected.

In 1965, Larner's book *The Addict in the Street*, which he wrote with Ralph Tefferteller, was published. Through interviews with certain heroin addicts, Larner and Tefferteller revealed how the addict conceived of himself and of the world in which he lived. The book was not an indictment but an attempt to allow readers to understand the problems and conditions that addicts were forced to face. As Larner pointed out, each addict speaking was emphatically telling of his desire to be like any average middle-class American. Indeed, he longed for a wife, children, and comfortable home. Larner wrote, "Marriage is sacred to him; family is sacred to him; likewise God, church, and country. I'm basically a decent person,

115

the addict insists, though the interviewer is not doubting him. This is the way I would lead my life . . . if only I weren't a drug addict. That's why I got to kick.—And he means it."[1]

Larner emphasized that society should change its methods as well as laws concerning addicts. He emphasized medical treatment and different attitudes by members of society so that the number of addicts would decline.

Larner contributed articles to several periodicals, including the *Nation, Paris Review, Partisan Review,* the *New Republic, Atlantic,* the *New Leader, Evergreen Review, Harper's,* and *Dissent,* among others.

In addition to his essays, short stories, and novels, he, together with Irving Howe, published *Poverty: Views from the Left* in 1968. Larner wrote the insightful *Nobody Knows: Reflections on the McCarthy Campaign of 1968,* which was published in 1970.

In 1972, he received an Oscar from the Academy of Motion Picture Arts and Sciences for best original screenplay for *The Candidate.* The movie featured Robert Redford.

Other books and numerous articles followed. His article "Initiation for Whitey: Notes on Poverty and Riot" illustrated his forceful style of writing.

SELECTED WORKS

The Addict in the Street (1964)
Poverty: Views from the Left (1968)

NOTE

1. Jeremy Larner and Ralph Tefferteller, *The Addict in the Street* (New York: Grove, 1964), 17.

REFERENCES

Larner, Jeremy. *Nobody Knows: Reflections on the McCarthy Campaign of 1968.* New York: Macmillan, 1970.

———. "I Didn't Get Mugged or Murdered but . . . ." *New Choices for Retirement Living* 34 (March 1994): 44–47.

———, and Irving Howe. *Poverty: Views from the Left*. New York: Morrow, 1968.

———, and Ralph Tefferteller. *The Addict in the Street*. New York: Grove, 1964.

Marx, Andy. "Jeremy Larner." *Variety*, July 26, 1993, 4.

Michael P. Lerner
(1943–)

Born on February 7, 1943, to Beatrice and Joseph Lerner in Newark, New Jersey, Michael Lerner was educated at Columbia University, from which he received his bachelor's degree in 1964, and at the University of California, Berkeley, from which he received his master's and doctorate in 1968 and 1972, respectively. He earned a second doctorate in 1977 from the Wright Institute.

Active in New Left politics, Lerner was indicted as a member of the group identified by the media as the "Seattle Seven." The charges against him were dismissed, however.

In 1969, Lerner was an assistant professor of philosophy at the University of Washington in Seattle. In 1971, his partner, Theirrie Cook, gave birth to their son. The same year he wrote "Mayday: Anatomy of the Movement" for *Ramparts*, a magazine that frequently published his work. The article concerned the protest march in Washington, D.C. In particular, it concerned the divisions within the organizational structure of Mayday that affected the Mayday march of 1971. Lerner severely criticized the organizers for failing to organize a massive demonstration.

In 1972, Lerner accepted a position at Trinity College in Hartford, Connecticut. The same year, Lerner, David Horowitz, and Craig Pyes coedited the book *CounterCulture and Revolution*. Lerner, an advocacy journalist as well as a professor of philosophy, believed that the New Left doctrine had not been presented coherently to the populace. Coincidentally, he believed and advocated that capitalism had to be explained more thoroughly before it could be replaced by socialism. He examined the issue in *The New Socialist Revolution: An Introduction to Its Theory and Strategy*, for instance, which was published in 1973, the year he became a contributing editor to *Ramparts*, a position that lasted until the magazine folded several years later.

In 1986, Lerner married Nan Fink and founded the magazine *Tikkun* as a forum for liberal Jewish viewpoints, even though many Jews had become more conservative by the mid-1980s as a result of Israeli politics and Ronald Reagan becoming president. The journal published articles about relations between African Americans and Jews, AIDS, abortion, Israel, modernism, psychiatry, and Zionism, among other topics. Contributors to the magazine included Annie Dillard, Todd Gitlin, Woody Allen, Marge Piercy, and John Judis, among others.

The same year Lerner wrote *Surplus Powerlessness: The Psychodynamics of Everyday Life—and the Psychology of Individual and Social Transformation*, in which he dealt with the "hidden" condition that inhibited Americans' fullest potential. According to Lerner, inequality existed among members of society primarily because of society's structure. For instance, most power in the United States was held by a few individuals, and most individuals had only a little power. This "powerlessness" on the part of the majority was real. "Surplus powerlessness" was the additional lack of power the majority imposed on itself; the majority of citizens did not exercise all of the options that were available to them and thus failed to gain power. In other words, most individuals, to a certain extent, failed to exert themselves; as a result, their lives at home and at work seemed monotonous or routine. This lack of hope on their part caused problems in the political arena as well, and, as Lerner pointed out, it was not power but powerlessness that caused corruption in society.

Lerner and Fink divorced in 1991. *Tikkun: To Heal, Repair and Transform the World: An Anthology*, which Lerner edited, was published in 1992 and contained articles that had been published in his journal. The articles focused on various topics from AIDS to Israel.

Lerner moved to New York City in 1992 and continued editing the magazine. A year later, he wrote *The Socialism of Fools: Anti-Semitism on the Left*, in which he explained that anti-Semitism existed because it was useful to those who wielded power, especially in exploitative or unequal societies. Lerner claimed that Jews had often appeared to have power over others because of their positions—from proprietors to physicians. He also claimed that anti-Semitism had never been a vital concern of the Left.

In 1996, he moved to San Francisco, where he helped form the Beyt TIKKUN synagogue. A year later he met Deborah Kohn, a Jewish theologian; they were married in 1998.

Lerner continued to publish his magazine as well as write books. In 2000, for instance, he wrote *Spirit Matters: Global Healing and the Wisdom of the Soul*, a basic introduction to spiritual thinking. In 2003, he wrote *Healing Israel/Palestine: A Path to Peace and Reconciliation*, which outlined how the two peoples could find peace. He wrote *The Left Hand of God: Taking Back Our Country from the Religious Right* in 2006, in which he expressed that politicians, particularly Democrats, should respond to a moral crisis that the majority of Americans were experiencing. Lerner outlined ways that society could change for the better.

In 2007, he edited the *Tikkun Reader: 20th Anniversary*, which contained numerous articles from the magazine.

SELECTED WORKS

CounterCulture and Revolution (with David Horowitz and Craig Pyes, 1972)

Surplus Powerlessness: The Psychodynamics of Everyday Life—and the Psychology of Individual and Social Transformation (1986)

The Politics of Meaning: Restoring Hope and Possibility in an Age of Cynicism (1996)

Healing Israel/Palestine: A Path to Peace and Recognition (2003)

The Left Hand of God: Taking Back Our Country from the Religious Right (2006)

Tikkun Reader: 20th Anniversary (editor, 2007)
Tikkun (founder)

REFERENCES

"Biographical Notes on Rabbi Lerner." www.tikkun.org/rabbi_lerner/bio .2008.
Fields-Meyer, Thomas. "This Year's Prophet." *New York Times Magazine*, June 27, 1993, SM28–30, 32, 36, 62.
Lerner, Michael, ed. *Tikkun: To Heal, Repair, and Transform the World: An Anthology*. Oakland, Calif.: Tikkun Books, 1992.
"Michael Lerner." *Newsmakers 1994*. Issue 4. Farmington Hills, Mich.: Gale Research,1994.

Dwight Macdonald
(1906–1982)

DWIGHT MACDONALD, A CRITIC WHO severely attacked Tom Wolfe's essay on the *New Yorker* in the mid-1960s, was born to Alice and Dwight Macdonald in New York City, in 1906, and attended the Collegiate School, the Barnard School for Boys, the Phillips Exeter Academy, and Yale University, from which he graduated in 1928. Although he majored in history, he wrote extensively for several university publications, including two he edited.

A year after he graduated, Macdonald was employed as a writer on the forthcoming Henry R. Luce publication *Fortune,* which appeared in 1930, and he wrote capitalistic articles concerning America's businesses and industries for seven years. He married Nancy Rodman in 1935.

In 1937, Macdonald made an ironic move to the newly revamped *Partisan Review.* Founded by William Phillips and Philip Rahv in 1934, the original *Review* was the foremost radical magazine for the creative Left. According to Frederick J. Hoftman, Charles Allen, and Carolyn F. Ubrick, "One of its chief aims was to provide a place for creative writing of leftist character, which was gradually being crowded out of *The New Masses* by the urgent demands of political and economic discussion. It began in New York City as a 'John Reed Club' publication—one of many established throughout the country to put the convictions of John Reed into practical action."[1]

The magazine combined with the *Anvil* in 1936 and became somewhat politically independent.

According to Hoftman, Allen, and Ubrick:

> The contents of the magazine changed. Disillusioned, the Party die-hards left, to concentrate their attention upon *The New Masses* and other orthodox journals. Contributions to *The Partisan Review* became . . . more definitely literary and critical, less polemic, the political discussions confined to the editorial columns or incorporated into the points of view of certain critics and essayists. The magazine . . . emphasized the "Trotskyist" position—world revolution, opposition to nationalism, and definite disapproval of Stalinist policies.[2]

While Macdonald was an editor and writer with the *Review*, he began writing for other publications, including the *New International*, the *Nation*, *Harper's*, and the *New Yorker*.

In 1943, Macdonald left the *Review* over a dispute concerning World War II. As he wrote in *Memoirs of a Revolutionist*, "After Pearl Harbor Rahv and Phillips had come to feel it was their war and their country, while I had remained disaffected. They wanted to reduce the magazine's political content and concentrate on literary criticism, while I wanted to continue the mixture as before."[3]

Macdonald published the first issue of *Politics* about six months later. This magazine, first a monthly then a quarterly, mirrored Macdonald's changing philosophy. From Marxism to empiricism, individualism, aestheticism, and moralism, he wrote articles that questioned people's inability to progress without their need or desire to harm. The magazine published writers such as Bruno Bettelheim, Andrea Caffi, Albert Camus, Lewis Coser, Paul Goodman, Peter Gutman, Victor Serge, Simone Weil, and George Woodcock. Unfortunately, the magazine failed to earn a profit, and Macdonald ceased publishing it in 1949. He was also more interested in writing than in publishing. His book *Henry Wallace, the Man and the Myth* had appeared a year before.

Macdonald and Nancy Rodman divorced in 1950. In 1951, he became a staff writer for the *New Yorker*, where he remained until 1966. In 1954, he and Gloria Lanier married. His book *The*

Ford Foundation: The Men and the Millions, which was published in 1956, was an expansion of several provocative articles he had written concerning the philanthropic organization. In addition to his articles for the *New Yorker,* which were ultimately collected and published in several volumes, he became the movie critic for *Esquire* in 1960, a position he held until 1966, when he became the magazine's political columnist.

Throughout much of the 1970s, Macdonald contributed to numerous magazines and taught in several universities. He died in 1982.

SELECTED WORKS

Politics (founder)
Henry Wallace, the Man and the Myth (1948)
The Ford Foundation: The Men and the Millions (1956)

NOTES

1. Frederick J. Hoftman, Charles Allen, and Carolyn F. Ubrick, *The Little Magazine: A History and a Bibliography* (Princeton, N.J.: Princeton University Press, 1947), 166–167.
2. Hoftman, Allen, and Ubrick, *The Little Magazine,* 168.
3. Dwight Macdonald, *Memoirs of a Revolutionist: Essays in Political Criticism* (New York: Farrar, Straus & Cudahy, 1957), 25.

REFERENCES

Macdonald, Dwight. *Memoirs of a Revolutionist: Essays in Political Criticism.* New York: Farrar, Straus & Cudahy, 1957.
Sumner, Gregory D. *Dwight Macdonald and the Politics Circle: The Challenge of Cosmopolitan Democracy.* Ithaca, N.Y.: Cornell University Press, 1996.
Whitfield, Stephen J. *A Critical American: The Politics of Dwight Macdonald.* Hamden, Conn.: Archon Books, 1984.
Wreszin, Michael. *A Rebel in Defense of Tradition: The Life and Politics of Dwight Macdonald.* New York: Basic Books, 1994.

Karl Marx (1818-1883)

KARL HEINRICH MARX WAS BORN on May 5, 1818, in Trier, Prussia (now Germany), to parents who were Jewish and descended from rabbis. His father, Heinrich, was baptized in the Evangelical Established Church, however, before his son was born.

Marx was encouraged by his father, a lawyer, to get a good education. When Marx completed high school in Trier, he attended the University of Bonn, where he studied history and Greek and Roman mythology for a year. In October 1836, he enrolled at the University of Berlin, where he studied philosophy and law. Although he had been baptized when he was six, he grew disillusioned with Christianity when he enrolled in a course that concerned the prophet Isaiah. The course was taught by Bruno Bauer, who proclaimed that the Christian Gospels were mere fantasies and that Jesus had not lived. Before Bauer was dismissed from the university in 1839, he had influenced numerous impressionable students, including Marx. Marx continued his studies at the University of Jena, where he received his doctorate in 1841.

Marx contributed to the *Rheinische Zeitung*, a liberal democratic newspaper that had been founded in Cologne. Before 1843, Marx had become editor of the newspaper and was writing editorials about societal and economic issues, including communism. Under Marx's editorship, the newspaper was outspoken—so much so that the authorities suppressed it a year later.

In 1843, Marx married Jenny von Westphalen. The couple moved to Paris, where he studied socialism and communism and edited, with Arnold Ruge, the short-lived review *Deutsch-Franzosische Jahrbucher* (German-French Yearbooks). Marx met Friedrich Engels, a contributor to the review, who was the son of a wealthy manufacturer. Although they would become collaborators, Marx offended the authorities by calling for an "uprising of the proletariat" and was subsequently expelled from France before they could contribute any collaborative articles to the review.

In 1845, Marx was living in Brussels. Engels, whose views were similar, also moved there. In 1845, they wrote *Die heilige Familie* (The Holy Family), which concerned Hegelian idealism and Bruno Bauer. They polemicized against Pierre-Joseph Proudhon, a French socialist, in *Misère de la Philosophie* (The Poverty of Philosophy), which was published in 1847.

One year later, Marx and Engels wrote the *Manifesto of the Communist Party* for the Communist League, which was based in London. The *Manifesto* discussed from a historical perspective the differences between the classes and asserted that communism would put an end to classes forever.

Marx moved to Paris before the Belgian authorities could expel him. Then he moved to Cologne, where he edited the controversial communist newspaper *Neve Rheinische Zeitung* in the midst of a revolution that was sweeping several countries in Europe. He advocated a war with Russia as well as the nonpayment of taxes, for which he was indicted. Although he was acquitted, he was expelled from Prussia.

In 1849, Marx and his family moved to London, where he joined the Communist League. In addition to writing speeches and articles that advocated revolutionary associations, he and Engels wrote articles and essays on other topics for periodicals.

Marx and his family were extremely poor. Indeed, in 1850 they were evicted for not paying their rent, and several of his children died during the next few years. Of course, to Marx, his family's financial plight could be blamed on the "bourgeois."

In 1851, Charles A. Dana, the managing editor of the *New York Daily Tribune*, asked Marx to become a correspondent. Dana, who had been introduced to Marx in Cologne several years earlier and had learned about Marx's ideas, realized that Marx would be perfect for the position. At the time, Horace Greeley's newspaper was championing utopian socialist ideas based on Fourierism. Marx agreed and immediately, together with Engels, wrote articles about Germany, Turkey, England, and other countries in Europe. They also wrote about Russia, India, China, and the United States. He and Engels contributed articles that discussed military affairs, elections in England, and capital punishment. Occasionally, whenever the articles contained elements of personalized reporting, Dana would run the articles as editorials. Marx's articles were not necessarily biased, however; he researched well the topics he discussed.

Charles Blitzer wrote, "More impressive than the breadth of his knowledge, the trenchancy of his wit, the felicity of his style—all of which were considerable—is the fact that in treating of current events Marx was able so consistently to distinguish the real from the illusory, the important from the trivial, the permanently significant from the momentarily impressive phenomena of his time."[1]

Marx and Engels contributed almost 500 articles to the newspaper. Marx wrote 350, while Engels wrote 125. They wrote more than ten together. Although certain scholars believe Marx lowered his standards as a philosopher by contributing to a newspaper, it should be mentioned that no matter what he wrote, his philosophy was emphatically stated. His writing for the *New York Daily Tribune*, for instance, not only revealed his philosophical beliefs but advocated certain reforms. For instance, in "Parliamentary Debates—The Clergy against Socialism—Starvation," Marx's attitude toward the philanthropists who supported the Ten Hours Bill of 1847 was vehemently cynical. He emphatically pointed out that the supporters were actually aristocratic landowners who were trying to get revenge for the abolition of the Corn Laws. Although Marx was writing about fact, his beliefs were revealed. Indeed, the reader immediately learned of his position toward the issue. Later in the article, he informed the reader of an unholy alliance between the established church and the aristocracy and revealed that he disliked this alliance. In the next to the last paragraph of the article, Marx mentioned that there was a pair of invisible, intangible, and silent despots in England that condemned individuals to their deaths or drove them from their land. According to Marx, the first was starvation; the second was forced emigration. Of course, Marx was acquainted with both. Perhaps this acquaintance not only enabled him to interpret information but enabled him to prophesy the numerous struggles that would occur between labor and industrialists and between industrialists and aristocrats.

Marx's earnings from his articles helped feed and clothe his family. When his articles were no longer needed eleven years later, however, his income was reduced substantially. If Engels as well as some relatives had not provided some financial assistance, Marx and his family would not have been able to live.

Marx, who had written a book on economic theory in 1859, became a major speaker for the International Working Men's Association in 1864. His efforts helped the organization increase its membership; by 1869, it had about eight hundred thousand members.

In 1870, when the Franco-German War broke out, Marx disagreed with certain constituencies in Germany. When the French armies were defeated, an insurrection occurred in Paris. The Paris Commune, as it was called, was supported by Marx, who, after it was crushed, proclaimed its significance in the address *Civil War in France*. As a result, Marx's name became synonymous with revolution, but he was opposed by certain constituencies inside the International Working Men's Association. Although these constituencies were defeated at the congress of the International in 1872, the organization languished for several years and was disbanded in 1876.

Marx withdrew from various movements. He was consulted several times by several activists, but he refused to become a participant in their groups. His health deteriorated, especially when his wife died in 1881, and he died on March 14, 1883.

SELECTED WORK

New York Daily Tribune (articles, 1851–1862)

NOTE

1. Henry M. Christman, ed., *The American Journalism of Marx and Engels, with an Introduction by Charles Blitzer* (New York: New American Library, 1966), xxvii.

REFERENCES

Bober, Mandell Morton. *Karl Marx's Interpretation of History*. Cambridge, Mass.: Harvard University Press, 1948.

Evans, Michael. *Karl Marx*. Bloomington: Indiana University Press, 1975.

Kamenka, Eugene. *The Portable Karl Marx*. New York: Penguin, 1983.

McLellan, David. *Karl Marx: His Life and Thought*. New York: Harper & Row, 1977.

Olsen, Richard E. *Karl Marx*. Boston: Twayne, 1978.

Payne, Robert. *Marx*. New York: Simon & Schuster, 1968.

Smulkstys, Julius. *Karl Marx*. New York: Twayne, 1974.

Wheen, Francis. *Karl Marx: A Life*. New York: Norton, 2000.

Wood, Allen W. *Karl Marx*. London: Routledge & Kegan Paul, 1981.

Henry Mayhew
(1812–1887)

HENRY MAYHEW WAS AN INVESTIGATING JOURNALIST who wrote about societal issues. In addition to his investigative reporting, which resembled advocacy journalism, he wrote humor, drama, and fiction. He also devoted time to editing and publishing magazines.

The son of Mary Ann and Joshua Mayhew, a London attorney, Mayhew was born in 1812. He attended Westminster School, but getting a formal education was not to his liking. He sailed to India, where he saw Calcutta. However, his stay was brief, and when he returned home, his father demanded that he work with him. Mayhew was not interested in learning about law.

Dissatisfied, he turned to chemistry, conducting experiments, one of which exploded, and literature and writing. In the 1830s, he and Gilbert à Beckett, an old friend from school, edited and published *Figaro in London*, which became a popular humorous illustrated weekly that had several imitators. The weekly lasted several years. Also in the 1830s, Mayhew edited another magazine, *The Thief*. This periodical was the first magazine to use reprints and clippings from other publications. *Punch; or, The London Charivari*, which Mayhew cofounded in 1841, was immediately successful. Unfortunately, when the magazine's financial support changed, its editorial policy changed, too. Frustrated, Mayhew severed his relationship with the publication. He realized he did not have to conform; instead, he became one of the best chroniclers of social conditions of his time. Like others of his day, he severely criticized laissez-faire philosophy and advocated for social reform.

Mayhew married Jane Jerrold in 1844. She was the daughter of Douglas Jerrold, who contributed to *Punch*. Eventually they had two children.

Although he helped found *Iron Times* in 1846, the newspaper ceased publication the same year. Mayhew turned to writing novels, from which he earned enough to support his family.

In 1849, Mayhew accepted a position with the *Morning Chronicle*, a newspaper, and investigated the poor of London. He wrote eighty-two articles that were published in the newspaper. He divided the poor into three categories: those who were willing to work, those who were not, and those who could not. He revealed how these people survived. He examined the poor who worked for manufacturing companies as well as the poor who worked for service companies. However, his articles grew increasingly critical of free trade. Eventually he left the *Morning Chronicle* but continued his investigation. His multivolume survey, which was incomplete, was titled *London Labour and the London Poor: A Cyclopaedia of the Condition and Earnings of Those That Will Work, Those That Cannot Work, and Those That Will Not Work* and was published in 1851. An in-depth analysis of the lowest classes of London society, the work was updated and published in newer editions over several years.

The Criminal Prisons of London and Scenes of Prison Life, which Mayhew considered his most important contribution, was published in 1862. Again Mayhew's powers of reporting were unsurpassed. His eye for details, no matter how minute, his unsentimental sympathy, his humor, his appetite for odd facts, and his ability to get information contributed to one of the most important social documents of the time.[1]

In 1864, after having lived in Germany for most of 1862 and having visited the country on numerous occasions, Mayhew published *German Life and Manners as Seen in Saxony at the Present Day: With an Account of Village Life—Town Life—Fashionable Life—Domestic Life—Married Life—School and University Life, &c., of Germany at the Present Time.*

In 1870, Mayhew edited *Only Once a Year*, a magazine that almost lived up to its name; it failed after a few issues.

Mayhew died in 1887.

SELECTED WORKS

London Labour and the London Poor: A Cyclopaedia of the Condition and Earnings of Those That Will Work, Those That Cannot Work, and Those That Will Not Work (1851)

The Criminal Prisons of London and Scenes of Prison Life (1862)

German Life and Manners as Seen in Saxony at the Present Day: With an Account of Village Life—Town Life—Fashionable Life—Domestic Life—Married Life—School and University Life, &c., of Germany at the Present Time (1864)

NOTE

1. David Daiches, ed., *The Penguin Companion to English Literature* (New York: McGraw-Hill, 1971), 357.

REFERENCES

Humpherys, Anne. *Travels into the Poor Man's Country: The Work of Henry Mayhew*. Athens: University of Georgia Press, 1977.

———. *Henry Mayhew*. Boston: Twayne, 1984.

H. L. Mencken
(1880–1956)

H. L. MENCKEN WROTE OPPOSING arguments for the United States getting involved in World War I in his column "The Free Lance," which appeared in the *Baltimore Evening Sun.*

Mencken was born in 1880 in Baltimore to an affluent, bourgeois German American family. He attended Professor Friedrich Knapp's Teutonic Institute and the Baltimore Polytechnic, where he excelled in chemistry and the natural sciences. He read voraciously both British and American literature and learned to play the piano. These continuing interests were later beneficial when he began writing essays and articles of criticism.

In 1899, Mencken obtained a job with the *Baltimore Morning Herald,* where he moved from one position to another, experiencing the responsibilities of the reporter as well as editor. In 1904, the *Morning Herald* was replaced by the *Evening Herald,* and Mencken rose to editor before the paper's demise two years later. He immediately moved to the *Baltimore Evening News* and then to the *Baltimore Sun.*

Mencken's writing was filled with agnosticism, elitism, and iconoclasm. These "isms" were reinforced by such thinkers and writers as Charles Darwin, Thomas Huxley, Friedrich Nietzsche, Herbert Spencer, William Sumner, and James Huneker. Mencken's literary efforts included not only news reports, editorials, reviews, features, and humor, but short stories, articles of criticism, and several researched studies such as the *Philosophy of Friedrich Nietzsche* and *The American Language*. Mencken was able to observe life around him and explain it vibrantly; indeed, color seemed to appear in every sentence he composed.

In 1908, Mencken began reviewing books for the *Smart Set*, a magazine published in New York City. Mencken's reputation as a critic spread. In 1914, he and the magazine's drama critic, George Jean Nathan, became editors, and together they produced much of the magazine's material. Mencken's contributions helped keep alive the spirit of the moral rebellion of the 1890s. According to Douglas C. Stevenson, "He defied the genteel assumption that American letters must be primarily Anglo-Saxon, optimistic, and morally uplifting. He ridiculed literary commercialism, dramatized the view that an essential function of art is to challenge accepted axioms, and conducted a boisterous onslaught against the 'snouters' who favored literary censorship."[1]

When his column "The Free Lance" appeared in 1911, Mencken gave the readers of Baltimore something they had never seen. Indeed, he ridiculed municipal politics, public works, language, certain persons within the community, and national and international affairs. His *Smart Set* articles would be altered to suit the column and vice versa. Eventually these articles and columns were collected and published.

When World War I began, Mencken's column was filled with venom. He attacked the pro-English Americans who distastefully ridiculed Germans who had come to America. His sentiment was so strong that he eventually became a partisan of Germany and was severely criticized by other members of the press. In 1915, the *Baltimore Sun* dropped his column, and the *Sun* soon sent Mencken abroad as a correspondent in the hope that his absence would quiet his critics. When he returned in 1917, however, criticism still confronted him. The United States was in the war, and Mencken's un-American attitude seemed unforgivable to his critics. When he published *A Book of Prefaces*, it was unduly and viciously attacked by reviewers. His book *The American Language* ultimately received critical acclaim and popularity, perhaps because the *Sun's* editors did not assign any stories to him or because the book was published in a calmer period.

For the next several years, Mencken wrote furiously for the *Sun*, *Smart Set*, *Atlantic Monthly*, and the *Nation*, attacking big business, big government, suppression, the "Red Scare," the Ku Klux Klan, education, sexual morality, and other issues. Between 1919 and 1927, the six-volume *Prejudices* series was published. Although many of the articles had appeared in one or more of the publications mentioned, this series did include additional articles.

In 1923, because of financial and editorial problems, *Smart Set* ceased publication. One month later, a new critical review backed by Alfred Knopf and edited by Mencken and Nathan appeared. Although the *American Mercury* was a better *Smart Set* in every respect, Nathan's and Mencken's opposing personalities caused Nathan to leave before the magazine was a year old. Mencken's publication contained literary criticism, which the readers enjoyed and respected, and political criticism, which the readers questioned. Mencken's attitudes toward politics, for example, seemed to change from month to month. His economics policy, which had been liberal to a certain extent, became conservative, and in the early 1930s, he supported Franklin Roosevelt but attacked Roosevelt's New Deal policies. Finally, he resigned from the magazine in 1933 and devoted the rest of his life to writing for the *Sun* and collecting his essays and letters, which were published in several volumes.

Mencken was working for the *Sun* when he suffered a stroke in 1948; he died eight years later.

SELECTED WORKS

"The Free Lance" (column)
Smart Set (editor)
American Mercury (editor)
Prejudices (six-volume series, 1919–1927)

NOTE

1. Douglas C. Stevenson, "Mencken, Henry Louis," *Dictionary of American Biography: Supplement Six 1956–1960*, ed. John A. Garraty (New York: Scribner's, 1980), 444.

REFERENCES

Bode, Carl. *Mencken*. Baltimore: Johns Hopkins University Press, 1986.

Douglas, George H. *H. L. Mencken: Critic of American Life*. Hamden, Conn.: Archon Books, 1978.

Fecher, Charles A. *Mencken: A Study of His Thought*. New York: Knopf, 1978.

Fitzpatrick, Vincent. *H. L. Mencken*. New York: Continuum, 1989.

Hobson, Fred C. *Mencken: A Life*. New York: Random House, 1994.

Kemler, Edgar. *The Irreverent Mr. Mencken*. Boston: Little, Brown, 1950.

Manchester, William. *Disturber of the Peace: The Life of H. L. Mencken*. New York: Harper, 1950.

Mayfield, Sara. *The Constant Circle: H. L. Mencken and His Friends*. New York: Delacorte, 1968.

Mencken, H. L. *Newspaper Days, 1899–1906*. New York: Knopf, 1941.

———. *Heathen Days, 1890–1936*. New York: Knopf, 1943.

Nolte, William Henry. *H. L. Mencken, Literary Critic*. Middletown, Conn.: Wesleyan University Press, 1966.

Rodgers, Marion Elizabeth. *Mencken: The American Iconoclast*. New York: Oxford University Press, 2005.

Stenerson, Douglas C. *H. L. Mencken: Iconoclast from Baltimore*. Chicago: University of Chicago Press, 1971.

Teachout, Terry. *The Skeptic: A Life of H. L. Mencken*. New York: HarperCollins, 2002.

Williams, W. H. A. *H. L. Mencken*. Boston: Twayne, 1977.

Cleveland Langston Moffett (1863–1926)

CLEVELAND LANGSTON MOFFETT was born on April 27, 1863, to Mary and William Moffett in Boonville, New York. After attending school in Boonville, he matriculated to Yale University and received his bachelor's degree in 1883. Moffett became a journalist for the *New York Herald*, where he remained until 1892. Then he joined the *New York Recorder*.

Moffett left the *New York Recorder* in 1894, after he translated Paul Bourget's *Cosmopolis: A Novel*, which had been published in French, in 1893. For the next several years, he contributed numerous articles to various publications, including newspapers, on many subjects, including science. For instance, he contributed "Life and Work in the Powder-Mills," which concerned the gunpowder industry, to *McClure's* in 1895; he contributed "The Marvels of Bicycle Making: A Visit to the Works of the Pope Tube Company" to *McClure's* in 1897. He also wrote books, including *The Mysterious Card*, published in 1896, and *Detective Stories from the Archives of the Pinkertons*, published in 1897.

Moffett married Mary Lusk, the daughter of a physician, in 1899 and started a family. He continued to write, however. He wrote a series of articles, "Careers of Danger and Daring," for *St. Nicholas*, a magazine for children. The series was then published in book form in 1901. Moffett also wrote plays, including *Money*

Talks, which was produced in 1906, and *Playing the Game*, which was produced in 1907, the year his article "Luxurious Newport" appeared in *Cosmopolitan Magazine*, and his novel *A King in Rags* was published. His play *The Battle: A Play of Modern New York Life* was produced in 1908 and lasted for another year. *Through the Wall*, another novel, was published in 1909. *For Better, for Worse*, another play, was produced in 1910. He contributed the article "Cassidy and the Food Poisons" to *Hampton's Magazine*. His play *Greater Than the Law* was produced in 1912. *The Land of Mystery*, another novel that had appeared in *St. Nicholas*, was published in 1913.

Moffett contributed "Steered by Wireless, and the Newest Terror in Warfare . . ." to *McClure's* in 1914, the year World War I erupted. He became an advocate for the United States and its allies, claiming that the United States had to prepare for the worst. He traveled to the front and wrote about what he observed. When he returned to the United States, he wrote *The Conquest of America: A Romance of Disaster and Victory: U.S.A., 1921 A.D.: Based on Extracts from the Diary of James E. Langston, War Correspondent of the "London Times"* in 1916. He actually depicted an invasion of the United States by a fictitious enemy. Finally, when the United States entered the war, he worked for the American Defense Society. In addition, he made numerous speeches and wrote about treason. He was also active in the Vigilantes, which had been organized to combat disloyalty. In 1917, in an attempt to quiet a speaker who was denouncing the United States and Great Britain, Moffett was arrested. Story after story about Moffett's arrest and its outcome appeared in the press. Moffett was against anyone who appeared to be unpatriotic, and he exercised his beliefs orally and in writing.

After the war, he wrote *Possessed*, a novel, which was published in 1920. He spent the rest of his life in California, where he adapted some of his books and plays for the movies, and in Paris, France. His novel *The Seine Mystery* was published in 1924.

Moffett died on October 14, 1926; he was sixty-three years old.

His last novel, *The Master Mind: A Detective Story*, was published in 1927.

SELECTED WORKS

New York Herald
New York Recorder
American Defense Society (trustee)
Vigilantes (chair)

REFERENCES

"Ask the President to Define Treason: Cleveland Moffett Says There Is Disloyalty in High and Low Places. How Far Can Speakers Go? Writer Also Declares That a Police Official Knows Germany Has Paid Money to Promote Sedition Here." *New York Times*, August 17, 1917, 7.

"Cleveland Moffett, Author, Dies in Paris: Journalist and Dramatist a Victim of Arterial Sclerosis at 63 after a Brief Illness." *New York Times*, October 16, 1926, 17.

"Disloyal Preaching Safe under the Law: No Way to Reach Seditious Orator through Federal Statute, Woods Says. Replies to Roosevelt: Cleveland Moffett Threatens to Break Up Another Meeting of Friends of Irish Freedom." *New York Times*, August 22, 1917, 4.

"Few German Papers Outspokenly Loyal: Security League Has Small Success Inducing Editors to Make "Profession of Faith." Some Notable Exceptions: Louis N. Hammerling Would Have Demanded a Declaration as Soon as the War Began." *New York Times*, August 20, 1917, 4.

"Moffett Arrested for Street Protest: Writer Charged Curb Speaker with Uttering Pro-German and Traitorous Remarks. Exonerated in Court: Magistrate Censures Policeman of German Birth and Advises Case Be Taken to Woods." *New York Times*, August 14, 1917, 1.

"Police Refuse to Help Moffett: Decline to Make Arrests at His Request for Street Abuse of England. Thousands Block Street: Speakers Abuse England, Sneer at the Vigilantes, and Praise La Follette." *New York Times*, August 23, 1917, 3.

"Seditious Orators to Be Prosecuted: Arrest of Cleveland Moffett Moves Defense Society to Plan Action. Police Promise to Help: Patrolmen Instructed to Arrest Curb Speakers Whose Remarks Appear to be Treasonable." *New York Times*, August 15, 1917, 4.

"Soap Box Orators Denounce England: Friends of Irish Freedom Refer to Cleveland Moffett as an Anglomaniac. Great Crowd Assembles:

Vigilantes Made No Attempt to Break Up Meeting, but Federal Officers Were on Guard." *New York Times*, August 19, 1917, 3.

"Soap Box Sedition to Feel Heavy Hand: City and Federal Authorities
Move to Stamp Out Propaganda of Treason. Work to Be County-Wide:
Police in 100 Cities Besides New York Asked to Act with Vigor against
Disloyal Utterances." *New York Times*, August 16, 1917, 7.

Willie Morris
(1934–1999)

WILLIE MORRIS WAS BORN TO Marion and Henry Rae Morris on November 29, 1934, in Jackson, Mississippi, and grew up in Yazoo City. In his autobiography, *North toward Home*, Morris explained what the name meant to him, "'Yazoo,' far from being the ludicrous name that others would take it, always meant for me something dark, a little blood-crazy and violent."[1]

Morris enjoyed the atmosphere of Yazoo; however, he believed the town had not stimulated his intellect. Like a character in a Mark Twain novel, he played practical jokes, got into trouble, and taunted "hell-fire and brimstone" preachers who tried to convert him. He played sports, especially baseball, and wrote sports stories for the *Yazoo Herald*. Later he worked in various capacities at a radio station.

In 1952, he entered the University of Texas at Austin, where he eventually matured. Playing catch-up, he read every book he could and tried to improve his writing. Although he wrote a column for the *Daily Texan*, his penchant for advocacy journalism did not become evident until he was named editor of the newspaper in his senior year. After attacking as well as exposing the oil industry, Morris had to fight the university not only to keep writing for the paper but to keep his position as editor. He wrote, "The attempt to censor *The Daily Texan* in 1956 involved not a displacement of dissent, but the running roughshod over it by real power, and the more

142 THE WRITERS AND EDITORS

sophisticated kind of criticism that served as its forum—the kind of wealth which still encourages the idea in America that anything can be bought, including culture."[2]

Morris received his degree in 1956 and, as a Rhodes Scholar, attended Oxford University, from which he received a second bachelor's degree and a master's degree. He married Celia Ann Buchan in 1958; they divorced in 1970.

Ronnie Dugger, whom Morris had known from his days at the University of Texas at Austin, asked Morris to return to Austin to take over the *Texas Observer*, a weekly newspaper Dugger had founded in 1955. Morris immediately responded. Although he was just twenty-five years old, he was not, in his words, "the same self-righteous, moralistic boy" he had been when he was editor of the *Daily Texan*. He wrote:

> I had the most earnest feelings that our little paper was somehow involved . . . in the great flow of history on this continent, and that to understand a place like Texas through its dissenters and its young rebels was to understand something of an older, vanished America; yet I also wished to be rooted in my own anxious time, a time when a new generation of young Americans would, for a tragically brief and poignant period, wield power.[3]

Morris, like Dugger, sustained the *Observer*'s fighting spirit. Almost every day he visited state legislators to learn what was on the agenda; he traveled throughout Texas to learn what people wanted from their legislators; he followed John F. Kennedy's 1960 campaign tour in Texas; he revealed the corruption within the state's governing bodies; he criticized the collusion between legislators and representatives of the petroleum industry; he attacked the John Birch Society as well as other right-wing organizations. In short, he not only presented the ills of Texas but advocated various means to get rid of them.

After three years, however, he was glad to see Dugger return. Morris resigned as editor and left Texas. For a brief period he lived in California, where he attended Stanford University. Within several months, he moved to New York City and obtained a position with *Harper's*. Morris became immersed in his work, so much so that he was advanced to executive editor in 1965. He changed the magazine by opening its pages to writers whose work he liked. According to Joan Babbitt, "The work of such new contributors as Larry King and William Styron infused vitality into a journal that had become pedestrian, stuffy, and uninspired."[4]

In 1967, at the age of thirty-two, Morris became the magazine's editor-in-chief, a position that had not been occupied by anyone that young in its 167 years. His autobiography, *North toward Home*, appeared the same year. The publishers approved of Morris's aggressive form of journalism, and he made the magazine one of the most discussed periodicals in the late 1960s. Indeed, the magazine offered readers lengthy and provocative pieces of writing, including David Halberstam's articles about Vietnam.

Without question, Morris, who published work by Marshall Frady, Midge Decter, Michael Harrington, and Robert Coles, helped the magazine's circulation. When he began to pay contributing editors $25,000 a year and writers at least $1,000 for an article, the magazine's financial position drastically changed, and William S. Blair, the newly appointed president, did not approve. Blair, a former advertising specialist, and John Cowles Jr., whose company owned *Harper's*, questioned Morris's business sense. In addition, Blair cared little for Morris's philosophy of journalism. Therefore, when Morris published the controversial essay "The Prisoner of Sex" by Norman Mailer, Blair confronted him about his handling of the magazine. Morris, who had fought for what he believed was right, resigned in 1971.

His book *Yazoo: Integration in a Deep-Southern Town* appeared later the same year. The book concerned the 1969 U.S. Supreme Court ruling that Morris's hometown be desegregated. Morris, through interviews with citizens of Yazoo, wrote of the town's dedicated efforts to make segregation a stigma of the past.

When *James Jones: A Friendship* appeared in 1978, it was attacked by critics for not being objective. Morris, who contributed articles, vignettes, and essays to such periodicals as the *Nation, Commentary, Dissent*, and the *New Yorker*, published a collection of magazine pieces under the title *Terrains of the Heart and Other Essays on Home* in 1981, a year after he had returned to Mississippi.

In 1983, his *Always Stand in Against the Curve and Other Sports Stories* and *The Courting of Marcus Dupree* appeared. The first book contained autobiographical essays about his days as a high school baseball player and the high school baseball tournament in Mississippi in 1952 in which his team was defeated. The second book presented the irony-rich story of football player Marcus Dupree. Morris mixed episodes from the early twentieth century with the history of Dupree's career. The book was a thorough examination of sports in the South.

Seven years later, he collected several essays about people and situations familiar to most readers—from spending Christmas at grandmother's house to an unconventional professor whose teaching methods left an indelible impression on a student—in the book *Homecomings*. Morris also wrote about the terror that gripped a small community after a heinous crime had been committed. He described familiar feelings, sights, smells, sounds, and tastes. Art by William Dunlap accompanied the essays. The same year he married JoAnne Prichard, an editor at the University Press of Mississippi.

In 1991, Morris published a series of essays about William Faulkner's life in Oxford, Mississippi, titled *Faulkner's Mississippi*. Photographs by William Eggleston accompanied the essays.

A year later, the insightful collection *After All, It's Only a Game* appeared. It contained three memoirs and three short stories that captured his fondness for baseball and football and his role in each. The stories concerned other sports, too, including basketball. Morris focused on simple, everyday aspects of sports to which most readers could relate.

In 1993, he wrote *New York Days*, a worthy sequel to his autobiographical *North toward Home*. The book was filled with nostalgia as he examined his days as editor of *Harper's* in the late 1960s. According to Morris, the magazine mirrored and interpreted the nation as a result of the various writers it published. Morris had encouraged writers to contribute literary journalism as well as advocacy journalism.

Another memoir, *My Dog Skip*, about his relationship with his dog and, of course, Yazoo, Mississippi, was published in 1995. The book was the basis for the film of the same title, which was released several years later. Morris served as a consultant on the film *Ghosts of Mississippi*. Three years later, he explored Mississippi's racist past in *The Ghosts of Medgar Evers: A Tale of Race, Murder, Mississippi, and Hollywood*, which concerned the murder of Medgar Evers by Ku Klux Klan member Byron De La Beckwith, the film *Ghosts of Mississippi*, and the failures of Hollywood.

Morris died on August 2, 1999. At that time, he had written, for the most part, two or three books; these were published post-humously.

SELECTED WORKS

Texas Observer (editor)
Harper's Magazine (editor-in-chief)
Terrains of the Heart and Other Essays on Home (1981)

NOTES

1. Willie Morris, *North toward Home* (Boston: Houghton Mifflin, 1967), 4.
2. Morris, *North toward Home*, 193.
3. Morris, *North toward Home*, 203.
4. Joan Babbitt, "Willie Morris," in *Dictionary of Literary Biography Yearbook: 1980*, ed. Karen L. Rood, Jean W. Ross, and Richard Ziegfeld (Detroit: Gale Research, 1981), 272.

REFERENCES

Bales, Jack. *Willie Morris: An Exhaustive Annotated Bibliography and a Biography*. Jefferson, N.C.: McFarland, 2006.
King, Larry L. *In Search of Willie Morris: The Mercurial Life of a Legendary Writer and Editor*. New York: Public Affairs, 2006.
Morris, Willie. *North toward Home*. Boston: Houghton Mifflin, 1967.
———. *New York Days*. Boston: Little, Brown, 1993.

Jack Newfield
(1939-2004)

JACK NEWFIELD, A SELF-TERMED American New Leftist, was influenced by Murray Kempton and Albert Camus in terms of style and ideas.

Newfield was born to Ethel and Phillip Newfield on February 18, 1939, in New York City. His father died when he was four years old. Newfield attended public schools, then matriculated to Hunter College (now Hunter College of the City University of New York), from which he graduated in 1961. Having written for the student newspaper while enrolled in college, Newfield wrote articles for *Commonweal*.

He worked briefly at the *New York Daily Mirror* and at *Women's Wear Daily*. Later, he worked as an editor at the *West Side News*, then as a reporter at the *New York Post*. Finally, in 1964, Newfield found employment as a reporter at the *Village Voice*, where he was promoted to senior editor before he left in 1988. Although he contributed numerous articles to other publications, including the *Evergreen Review*, the *Nation*, *New York*, *Partisan Review*, and *Playboy*, his writing for the *Village Voice* concerned civil rights, lead poisoning, hippies, the 1968 Democratic Convention, Students for a Democratic Society, Vietnam, Nelson Rockefeller, John Lindsay, Theodore Sorensen, the media, poor whites, the legal system, Norman Mailer, Ralph Nader, Robert Kennedy, and any other politician, writer, or issue that affected him or his beliefs.

An advocate who believed in morality, laws, and equal justice, Newfield criticized the wrongs of American society but also praised what he found to be good in America.

His first book, *A Prophetic Minority*, which discussed the rise of the New Left, was published in 1966. His critically acclaimed analysis of Robert Kennedy, *Robert Kennedy: A Memoir*, appeared in 1969. The book was not a biography per se but rather a personal testament that criticized as well as praised. Newfield detailed the insurgencies of the 1960s that Robert Kennedy eventually grew to understand and confidently pronounced as societal necessities.

Newfield produced a collection of his articles in 1971. Titled *Bread and Roses Too: Reporting about America*, the articles were grouped according to the issues discussed or ideas advocated. One of the articles exemplified Newfield's ability to foster a certain mood and captured his attitudes toward President Richard Nixon after a televised presidential address.

In 1972, with Jeff Greenfield, he wrote the popular *A Populist Manifesto: The Making of a New Majority*. The writers wrote in the preface:

> This manifesto is a platform for a movement that does not yet exist. It is not a book about the 1972 campaign, or a blue-print for Utopia in 2001.
>
> It is instead an effort to return to American politics the economic passions jettisoned a generation ago. Its fundamental argument is wholly unoriginal: some institutions and people have too much money and power, most people have too little, and the first priority of politics must be to redress that imbalance.[1]

The authors then elaborated on issues such as banking, insurance, utilities, taxes, regulatory agencies, land reform, the media, crime, health, unions, and foreign policy, and they subsequently advocated reforms.

Newfield also wrote the arresting and controversial book *Cruel and Unusual Justice* in 1974. With Paul Du Brul, he wrote *The Abuse of Power: The Permanent Government and the Fall of New York* in 1977. In 1984, he wrote the insightful book *The Education of Jack Newfield*.

He left the *Village Voice* in 1988 and became an investigative reporter and columnist at the *New York Daily News*. He and Wayne Barrett criticized the men who surrounded Mayor Ed Koch in the penetrating journalistic study *City for Sale: Ed Koch and the Betrayal of New York*, which was published in 1989. The authors claimed that these men were as crooked as a dog's hind legs. Newfield and Barrett disclosed that Koch had turned over parts of City Hall to those he said he opposed. The book was not necessarily a balanced report, but the authors' claims were accurate.

Newfield left the *New York Daily News* and joined the *New York Post* in 1991, for which he contributed a column. When Rupert Murdoch purchased the paper in 2001, Newfield and his column were let go.

In 1995, Newfield wrote *Only in America: The Life and Crimes of Don King*, in which he depicted King's rise from a numbers racketeer who killed a gambler in a fight to an ex-con who became a promoter of boxing matches. Newfield's biography was revealing, to say the least.

In *Somebody's Gotta Tell It: The Upbeat Memoir of a Working-Class Journalist*, which was published in 2002, Newfield examined his own life from growing up in Brooklyn to becoming an advocate for those who seemed to be overlooked by the movers and shakers of society. A year later *The Full Rudy: The Man, the Mayor, the Myth* was published.

Newfield died of cancer on December 20, 2004.

SELECTED WORKS

A Prophetic Minority (1966)
Bread and Roses Too: Reporting about America (1971)
A Populist Manifesto: The Making of a New Majority (with Jeff Greenfield, 1972)
Cruel and Unusual Justice (1974)
The Abuse of Power: The Permanent Government and the Fall of New York (with Paul Du Brul, 1977)
The Education of Jack Newfield (1984)

City for Sale: Ed Koch and the Betrayal of New York (with Wayne Barrett, 1989)
The Full Rudy: The Man, the Mayor, the Myth (2003)

NOTE

1. Jack Newfield and Jeff Greenfield, *A Populist Manifesto: The Making of a New Majority* (New York: Praeger, 1972), ix.

REFERENCES

Newfield, Jack. *The Education of Jack Newfield*. New York: St. Martin's, 1984.
———. *Somebody's Gotta Tell It: The Upbeat Memoir of a Working-Class Journalist*. New York: St. Martin's, 2002.

George Orwell
(1903-1950)

GEORGE ORWELL WROTE ADVOCACY as well as literary journalism in addition to allegorical novels. Because of his educational background, his experiences in the slums of London and Paris, and his experiences in the Spanish Civil War, he was able to depict his socialist philosophy in various forms of expression, including short stories, articles, essays, and exposes.

Although born in Bengal, India, in 1903, Eric Arthur Blair, better known as George Orwell, was reared in England, his parents' homeland. His parents were not wealthy, but they sent him to St. Cyprians, an expensive school, where he became aware of social class differences. Later he attended Wellington, then Eton, both private schools. In 1922, he passed the examinations for the Indian Imperial Police and became assistant superintendent of police in Rangoon, Burma. After five years, he realized that such a career was not rewarding.

Returning to England in 1927, soon he was tramping through the East End of London, where the poor, the despised, and the thieves congregated and barely survived. Whether Orwell was escaping his own social class, had read *The People of the Abyss*, or had been inspired to see for himself what Charles Dickens had described in that work, he made numerous visits during the next several years. In 1928, he moved to Paris; London was too expensive. During the next two years he wrote numerous short stories and articles as well as two novels. The stories and novels were rejected, but several of his articles were eventually published in *Progres Civique* and *Monde*.

Before he returned to his parents' home in Southwald in 1929, Orwell visited the worst sections of Paris. He combined his observations of Paris with those he had made of London, and from late 1929 to 1933, he added information and revised his manuscript. When *Down and Out in Paris and London* was published in 1933, the name George Orwell, one of four Blair had suggested to the publisher, appeared on the cover. Readers immediately realized that Orwell had written about actual occurrences in a novelistic fashion. The book was instantly successful.

From 1930 to 1935, he contributed book reviews, articles, and poetry to *Adelphi* and other magazines, meanwhile supporting himself by teaching in private schools. His second book, *Burmese Days*, was finished in December 1933, just before he entered the hospital. Although he recovered from an apparent case of pneumonia, he did not return to teaching. Instead, he devoted his time to writing and working in a bookstore. *Burmese Days* was followed by *A Clergyman's Daughter* in 1935. His third novel, *Keep the Aspidistra Flying*, appeared a year later.

The Road to Wigan Pier, a serious study of poverty and unemployment in England, was commissioned by Victor Gollancz in 1936. According to Richard H. Rovere:

> The first half is exactly that. . . . The second part is an examination of socialism as a remedy. It was perhaps the most rigorous examination that any doctrine has ever received at the hands of an adherent. It was so tough, so disrespectful, so rich in heresies that Mr. Gollancz . . . published the book only after writing an introduction that could not have been more strained and apologetic if he had actually been a Wesleyan minister who for some improbable reason found himself the sponsor of a lecture by George Bernard Shaw on the Articles of Religion.[1]

Orwell served as a journalist, then as a soldier in the Spanish Civil War. While fighting fascism, he was wounded and subsequently brought back to England. What he had experienced and witnessed transformed his political philosophy from a weak belief in socialism to a strong one. In 1938, his *Homage to Catalonia* was published. A personal memoir of the war, the book was a forceful, descriptive account of a senseless social and political revolution. Although the book did not sell well, it contained the philosophy that he later presented in the allegory *Animal Farm* and in the dystopian *1984*.

Homage to Catalonia was characteristic of his personal style of reporting. Using the first-person point of view quite effectively, Orwell described the absurdities that seemingly plague every war. By speaking as a participant, Orwell enhanced his credibility as an observer. Orwell used anecdotes to convey the realities of war; more specifically, of the war he witnessed. Dialogue and scene-by-scene construction were used to present the truth as he saw it.

Orwell accurately described numerous incidents in the Spanish Civil War. His work was an undeniable portrait of what a soldier experienced.

In 1940, *Inside the Whale, and Other Essays* was published. For the rest of his life, Orwell wrote novels, essays, book reviews, articles, educational programs for the British Broadcasting Corporation, editorials, and World War II accounts. His writing appeared in *Horizon, Tribune, Time and Tide, New Statesman, Partisan Review, Observer*, and other publications. In 1946, *Critical Essays* was published. Four years later, the year he died of tuberculosis, *Shooting an Elephant, and Other Essays* was published.

Several books were published after his death, including *England Your England and Other Essays* and *A Collection of Essays*, which were published in 1953 and 1954, respectively.

SELECTED WORKS

Down and Out in Paris and London (1933)
The Road to Wigan Pier (1936)
Homage to Catalonia (1938)
Inside the Whale, and Other Essays (1940)
Critical Essays (1946)

Shooting an Elephant, and Other Essays (1950)
England Your England and Other Essays (1953)

NOTE

1. George Orwell, *The Orwell Reader*, with an introduction by Richard W. Rovere (New York: Harcourt, Brace & World, 1956), xv–xvi.

REFERENCES

Atkins, John Alfred. *George Orwell: A Literary and Biographical Study.* New York: Ungar, 1955.
Bowker, Gordon. *Inside George Orwell.* New York: Palgrave Macmillan, 2003.
Crick, Bernard. *George Orwell: A Life.* Boston: Little, Brown, 1980.
Fyvel, Tosco. *George Orwell, a Personal Memoir.* New York: Macmillan, 1982.
Stansky, Peter, and William Abrahams. *The Unknown Orwell.* New York: Knopf, 1972.
———. *Orwell, the Transformation.* New York: Knopf, 1980.
Taylor, D. J. *Orwell: the Life.* New York: Holt, 2003.
Woodcock, George. *The Crystal Spirit: A Study of George Orwell.* Boston: Little, Brown, 1966.

Thomas Paine
(1737–1809)

Born in 1737 to a lower-class Quaker family in Thetford, Norfolk, England, Thomas Paine attended Thetford Grammar School. When he was sixteen, he left home by ship and sailed as far as London, where he became an apprentice to a staymaker. London at this time was, according to Howard Fast, "as close an approximation of hell as is possible to create on this earth."[1] Fast described the city in these terms:

> The enclosure laws of the previous two centuries had created a huge landless population that gravitated . . . mostly toward London, to form a half-human mob, not peasants, not craftsmen—the first tragic beginnings of a real working class. . . . Starvation, thievery, murder, and drunkenness were the order of the day. The section where these people lived was known as the Gin Mill; gin was their only escape. No doubt, when Paine went into the Gin Mill, when he sought to escape staymaking through that valley of hopelessness, gin was his surcease too. He went as low as the people, suffered with them, attempted their avenues of escape, and thereby came to understand them.[2]

Paine learned of Newtonianism from attending philosophical lectures given by Benjamin Martin, James Ferguson, and others. He was also influenced by classical antiquity, which was commonly used by deists when confronted by churchmen. For instance, if

Paine was questioned whether men could live morally without Christianity, he would mention that Aristotle, Plato, and Socrates had lived before Christ, yet they had signs of nobility. Another influence was freemasonry's relationship to the religions of ancient Egypt, the Persians, and the Druids. These four influences—Quakerism, Newtonianism, classicism, and the early Eastern religions and freemasonry—formed four major religious premises: (1) nature is divine, (2) nature is law, (3) man must be a part of this divine revelation, and (4) an attempt must be made to reestablish man's relations with this natural law in politics and religion.[3] Paine's political philosophy grew from these premises.

After numerous jobs in various places, Paine got a job as a tax collector. He disliked the position, however, and returned to staymaking. He tried other trades such as cabinetmaking and cobbing, but despair followed him.

From 1768 to 1774, Paine was an excise officer at Lewes, Sussex. He was dismissed for addressing Parliament on behalf of the excisemen who had requested higher wages. Since he had lost his business and was in debt, he borrowed enough money to sail to America.

Benjamin Franklin, whom Paine had met in London, helped him find employment. Paine worked as an editor for Robert Aitken, the publisher of the *Pennsylvania Magazine*. Almost immediately, Paine's advocacy journalism earned him a reputation as one of the foremost writers of his day. In addition to writing antislavery essays, he wrote for the revolutionary cause. Within the revolutionary climate, Paine was at ease; he knew that his hour had arrived and that his political and religious philosophies would ignite the fuse of perhaps the greatest power ever witnessed.

Paine served as editor of the *Pennsylvania Magazine* for approximately eighteen months. In 1776, he published *Common Sense*, which influenced the makers of the Declaration of Independence, and the first number of *The Crisis*, which encouraged the soldiers of the Revolutionary War. In 1780, he published *Public Good*, in which he urged the nation to become the owner of western lands claimed by Virginia. During 1782 and 1783, he wrote six letters for the *Providence Gazette*, in which he defended taxation of Rhode

Island by the federal government. In 1791, after having returned to England, he published the first and second parts of *The Rights of Man*, which was a reply to Edmund Burke's critical *Reflections on the French Revolution*. *The Rights of Man* advocated that England needed a revolution similar to that which had occurred in France. Paine was charged with sedition; before his trial, however, he escaped to France, where he wrote the third part of *The Rights of Man*. In 1793, he wrote the first part of *Age of Reason*; the second part appeared three years later.

Although *Common Sense, The Crisis, The Rights of Man*, and the *Age of Reason* were perhaps his most important writings, Paine also wrote *Dissertation on the First Principles of Government, Dissertations on Government, the Bank, and Paper Money, Decline and Fall of the English System of Finance, Letter to Washington, Agrarian Justice, Discourse to the Theophilandthropists, Letters to the Citizens of the United States*, and *Reply to the Bishop of Llandoff*.

According to Harry Hayden Clark, Paine assumed that men were by nature altruistic. He was convinced that every man was endowed by the creator with certain natural rights. He believed in rational principles to promote progress. He was convinced that these principles had to be in the form of a constitution. He assumed that in order to promote the good for all there had to be a governmental body to which the people had access.[4] Paine, of course, was not the first political philosopher. Indeed, Voltaire, Locke, and Milton, to name a few, preceded him. Paine's writing was different, however, as Fast mentioned, "They wrote abstractly of the pattern of change; Paine wrote realistically of the method of change. They were philosophers who created political philosophy; Paine was a revolutionist who created a method for revolution. They moved men to thought; Paine moved men to thought and action. They dealt with theory and ideals; Paine dealt with the dynamics of one force playing against another."[5]

In *Common Sense*, Paine tried to persuade the reader that America had the capabilities to break with England. Although his points were abrupt, they had an impact.

Excerpts of *Common Sense* were printed in newspapers and, as a result, Paine's beliefs about "independence" united Americans throughout the colonies. Without question, the popular pamphlet helped initiate the Revolutionary War and served as a model for the Declaration of Independence, which was written several months later.

Paine died in 1809.

Selected Works

Pennsylvania Magazine (editor)
Common Sense (1776)
The Crisis (1776)
Public Good (1780)
The Rights of Man (1791–1792)
Age of Reason (1793–1796)

Notes

1. Howard Fast, ed., *The Selected Work of Tom Paine: Set in the Framework of His Life* (New York: Duell, Sloan & Pearce, 1945), ix.
2. Fast, ed., *The Selected Work of Tom Paine*, ix–x.
3. Harry Hayden Clark, *Thomas Paine: Representative Selections, with Introduction, Bibliography, and Notes* (New York: American Book, 1944), xv–xvi.
4. Clark, *Thomas Paine*, xxxiv–li.
5. Fast, ed., *The Selected Work of Tom Paine*, xii.

References

Aldridge, Alfred Owen. *Man of Reason: The Life of Thomas Paine*. Philadelphia: Lippincott, 1959.
Best, Mary Agnes. *Thomas Paine: Prophet and Martyr of Democracy*. New York: Harcourt, Brace, 1927.
Fast, Howard. *Citizen Tom Paine*. New York: Duell, Sloan & Pearce, 1943.
Foner, Eric. *Tom Paine and Revolutionary America*. New York: Oxford University Press, 1976.

Fruchtman, Jack. *Thomas Paine: Apostle of Freedom*. New York: Four Walls Eight Windows, 1994.

Keane, John. *Tom Paine: A Political Life*. Boston: Little, Brown, 1995.

Larkin, Edward. *Thomas Paine and the Literature of Revolution*. New York: Cambridge University Press, 2005.

Nelson, Craig. *Thomas Paine: Enlightenment, Revolution, and the Birth of Modern Nations*. New York: Penguin Books, 2007.

Wilson, Jerome D. *Thomas Paine*. Boston: Twayne, 1989.

Woodward, William E. *Tom Paine: America's Godfather, 1737–1809*. New York: Dutton, 1945.

Westbrook Pegler
(1894–1969)

WESTBROOK PEGLER WAS BORN TO Frances and Arthur Pegler in Minneapolis in 1894. One of the most critical columnists of the 1900s, he grew up in Chicago, where he graduated from grade school, but he dropped out of Lane Technical School after a year and a half.

When he was sixteen, he was employed as an office boy by the United Press, where he eventually became a telephone reporter. Although he enjoyed reporting, his parents advised him to return to school. Enrolling at Loyola Academy, Pegler learned Latin, English composition, and even drawing. But he yearned for a newsroom and left after two or three semesters. He worked for a year for the International News Service, which merged with the United Press.

In 1913, he worked for a newspaper in Des Moines, then returned to the United Press offices, first in New York City, then in St. Louis, and finally in Dallas, where he worked as a reporter and bureau manager. Three years later he became a foreign correspondent and moved to London. When the United States entered World War I, he became a war correspondent with the American Expeditionary Force, which censored his stories. Eventually, dissatisfaction forced him to resign and enlist in the navy.

When the war ended, he returned to the United Press in New York City, for which he wrote and edited sports from 1919 to 1925. Pegler's sports reporting earned him a reputation. Like Damon Runyon, he presented minute but interesting details of every sports event. However, Pegler did not dwell on the team that won the game; he wrote about the people who filled the stadium, including what they drank during the game. Pegler also wrote about his beliefs toward issues of the time, including Prohibition and politics. It was not uncommon for him to incorporate sports analogies whenever he presented his opinions about topical issues.

Pegler married Julia Harpman, a reporter, in 1922. Three years later he moved to the *Chicago Tribune*, where he was highly paid for his sports reporting. As his commentaries on the hilarious or unusual side of sports and sports figures were read, Pegler's reputation spread. In 1932, he was sent by the *Tribune* to Washington to write about politics and politicians. Pegler found his ultimate purpose in life. In 1933, as a result of his political reportage, he was hired by the Scripps-Howard organization to write a column. "Fair Enough" captured the attention of both readers and newspaper professionals, and caused numerous investigations into labor unions. For instance, in one of his columns, he exposed William Bioff, a Hollywood union official, as an extortionist; when authorities were convinced that Pegler's accusations were true, Bioff was sentenced. A collection of his essays, *'T Ain't Right*, was published in 1936. This was followed by another collection, *The Dissenting Opinions of Mister Westbrook Pegler*, in 1938. In other columns, Pegler exposed George Scalise, the president of the Building Service Employees' International Union, as an extortionist and former criminal. Scalise was eventually sentenced. Pegler received the Pulitzer Prize for his efforts in 1941.

In addition to attacking labor union bosses, Pegler exposed or criticized other people and causes, including Elliot Roosevelt and John Hartford, Franklin and Eleanor Roosevelt, Upton Sinclair, Frank Sinatra, and Huey Long, as well as Nazism, communism, the income tax system, and the Newspaper Guild. Favoritism was not in his vocabulary; indeed, if he saw something wrong, he exposed and criticized it in his column. *George Spelvin, American, and Fireside Chats*, another collection of essays, was published in 1942.

In 1944, he moved to the *Journal-American* and began writing "As Pegler Sees It." Although similar to his earlier column, he intermittently used the character named George Spelvin, American, or a member of George's family, to present information. These columns, often humorous and satiric, both informed and entertained readers.

Several of his George Spelvin columns were similar to his sports reportage in that he used techniques and devices found in fiction. Usually, the column presented his opinion in a satiric manner. Pegler's use of satire was effective in the sense that it allowed the reader to understand his position on an issue. If he had presented this position in a mere editorial, the message, in all likelihood, would have been forgotten sooner.

In 1949, Pegler severely ridiculed Quentin Reynolds, a war correspondent and magazine writer who had reviewed a biography of Heywood Broun that had described how Broun had read a column by Pegler and had become fatally ill. Pegler had not particularly cared for Reynolds's review or his personality. Consequently, in perhaps one of his most scathing columns, Pegler belittled Reynolds. Reynolds sued Pegler for libel and won. Nonetheless, Pegler remained as critical as ever. From Harry Truman to his own employer, William Randolph Hearst Jr., no one was above reproach.

Pegler's wife, Julia, died in 1955; Pegler married Pearl Doane four years later. This marriage did not last, however, and he married Maude Towart, his secretary, in 1960.

Pegler kept attacking and criticizing, until the Hearst organization, which included King Features Syndicate, announced in 1962 that it would not publish another column. Pegler wrote for *American Opinion* as well as other publications until he died in 1969.

SELECTED WORKS

"Fair Enough" (column)
"As Pegler Sees It" (column)
'T Ain't Right (1936)
The Dissenting Opinions of Mister Westbrook Pegler (1938)
George Spelvin, American, and Fireside Chats (1942)

References

Farr, Finis. *Fair Enough: The Life of Westbrook Pegler*. New Rochelle, N.Y.: Arlington House, 1975.

Pilat, Oliver. *Pegler: Angry Man of the Press*. Boston: Beacon, 1963.

Richard Reeves (1936-)

Born in New York City on November 28, 1936, to Dorothy and Furman Reeves, Richard Reeves attended Stevens Institute of Technology, from which he received his degree in 1960. After a year of working at Ingersoll-Rand Company as an engineer, he abandoned the profession for which he was educated and became an editor of the *Phillipsburg Free Press*.

Reeves married Carol Wiegand in 1959 and started a family. Four years later, he left the *Phillipsburg Free Press* and accepted a position as a reporter at the *Newark News*, where he stayed two years. His writing, which was concise, accurate, and arresting, enabled him to obtain a position with the *New York Herald Tribune*, then the *New York Times*, for which he worked as chief political correspondent. His experience in political reporting eventually led him to write articles and several books that exposed as well as analyzed politicians and the political process. In 1971, when he and Carol divorced, he became an editor of *New York*, a position he held until 1977. In addition, he contributed a column to *Harper's* in the early 1970s. He served as national editor at *Esquire* from 1977 to 1979, the year he married Catherine O'Neill. Then he became a syndicated columnist. He also joined the editorial advisory board of the *Washington Monthly*.

Reeves, a political columnist of national magnitude, wrote the investigative analytical study *A Ford, Not a Lincoln*, which was published in 1975. Reeves explored the first one hundred days of the Ford presidency. Reeves failed to hide his biases in his study, but the book was nonetheless a well-written and informative document of immense importance. In 1977, his book *Convention* was published. Concerned with the shenanigans of presidential conventions, Reeves stripped away the gloss and glitter from the 1976 Democratic Convention in New York City and revealed in vignettes the carnival atmosphere that was typical of any political convention. Reeves used descriptive vignettes of scenes and characters, and incorporated actual dialogue spoken by the numerous participants.

American Journey: Traveling with Tocqueville in Search of Democracy in America, in which Reeves traced Alexis de Tocqueville's steps to learn what American democracy had become, was published in 1982. Reeves compared Tocqueville's journals with his own to determine whether American democracy was still the same and whether it was still working. Reeves's findings were basically the same as Tocqueville's: "It does work. . . . The glory and the frustration of American democracy is that greatness is defined by each American—and that's the way we meant it to be."[1]

In 1985, he examined quite critically the conservative philosophy of Ronald Reagan in *The Reagan Detour: Conservative Revolutionary*. Reeves deplored Reagan's conservative belief that the best way to increase investment was to let the wealthy keep more of their money. He believed that this would reduce the bargaining power of the poor. Reeves also discussed three areas of opportunity for the Democrats: (1) the weaknesses of Reaganism, (2) the decline of America's industrial competitiveness, and (3) problems with the nation's foreign policy. Unfortunately, Reeves failed to offer solutions to the problems he discussed; he did, however, offer suggestions. The same year he published the insightful *A Passage to Peshawar: Pakistan between the Hindu Kush and the Arabian Sea*, based on his journey through the Asian country. Reeves recorded his reactions to the country and its people. As a Westerner with certain biases, he found the culture difficult to comprehend and accept. Nonetheless, through a series of interwoven essays, Reeves provided the reader with a glimpse of the country's problems as it attempted to retain some seemingly antiquated customs in the midst of progress.

Reeves returned to a familiar subject in *President Kennedy: Profile of Power*, which was published in 1993. Although the biography fell short of capturing the human dimensions of Kennedy, the man, it was an engaging and even elegant recounting of the Kennedy era. In short, Reeves succeeded in presenting the president as he actually was—strong and courageous, with certain flaws in his character.

Running in Place: How Bill Clinton Disappointed America, which was published in 1996, concerned the first four years of Clinton's presidency. Reeves expressed that President Clinton and his administration failed to inspire the American people and consequently were disappointments.

In 1998, *What the People Know: Freedom and the Press*, in which Reeves examined the future of journalism, was published. Reeves's opinions about the media focused on news organizations and their willingness to sacrifice hard news for trivial and sensationalistic stories in an effort to generate greater profits.

Reeves examined another president in *President Nixon: Alone in the White House*, published in 2001. The biography was based on thousands of documents, including Nixon's writings, as well as interviews with the president's associates. The book was praised by critics for its insight.

In 2005, *President Reagan: The Triumph of Imagination* was published. Reeves focused on the eight years President Reagan was in the White House. The book was based on documents and interviews. Although the eight years were accurately depicted, Reeves's biases against Reagan's political policies were also present, which bothered critics.

Two years, later he examined the life of Ernest Rutherford, a physicist, in *A Force of Nature: The Frontier Genius of Ernest Rutherford*.

In addition to writing, Reeves taught at several universities, including Columbia University in New York City and the University of Southern California.

SELECTED WORKS

Column (syndicated)
A Ford, Not a Lincoln (1975)
Convention (1977)
American Journey: Traveling with Tocqueville in Search of Democracy in America (1982)
The Reagan Detour: Conservative Revolutionary (1985)
President Kennedy: Profile of Power (1993)
Running in Place: How Bill Clinton Disappointed America (1996)
President Nixon: Alone in the White House (2001)
President Reagan: The Triumph of Imagination (2005)

NOTE

1. Richard Reeves, *American Journey: Traveling with Tocqueville in Search of Democracy in America* (New York: Simon & Schuster, 1982), 357.

REFERENCES

Reeves, Richard. *Family Travels: Around the World in Thirty (or So) Days.* Kansas City, Mo.: Andrews & McMeel, 1997.
"Richard Reeves" website. www.richardreeves.com (2008).

Robin Reisig (1944-)

ROBIN REISIG WAS BORN in 1944 and was reared in a comfortable suburb of Detroit. Attending private schools in Bloomfield Hills, she matriculated at Wellesley, a New England Ivy League college, where she worked for the school newspaper. During the summers, she worked for several newspapers, including the *Free Press* in Detroit and the *Patriot Ledger* in Boston.

Upon graduation, Reisig moved to the South, where she encountered numerous individuals who were less fortunate in life than she. She was hired as a reporter by the *Southern Courier* and covered local events, including murder trials. Although Reisig matured as a reporter, she grew tired of the South.

Reisig applied to the Columbia Journalism School and was accepted. By the time she graduated, she was determined not to work at a newspaper. As a result of a friend's encouragement, however, she was invited to contribute several articles to the *Village Voice*, which she gladly accepted. Her first article, which concerned the telephone company, was published in 1969. Her second article concerned women who defied bars restricted to men. Reisig contributed other articles, but most took several weeks to research and write. Her income was strained as a result. After a year, she was assigned stories that required even more time to investigate and write. One of these articles, "The Vets and Mayday," which was published in the *Village Voice* in 1971, described the People's

Lobby Week—specifically, the staged operation called Dewey Canyon III, in which veterans carried out a simulated search-and-destroy mission among the citizens of Washington, D.C. Reisig acknowledged that the veterans' demonstration greatly affected members of the Senate Foreign Relations Committee. This article, like others she wrote, was an example of advocacy journalism that appeared in the *Village Voice* and other periodicals during this period.

Reisig contributed lengthy articles to the paper, but she was not paid nearly enough. After all, she had invested a considerable amount of time on each story. Nonetheless, she contributed to the *Village Voice* with the hope that she would be offered a staff position. She wrote about prostitution as well as what it was like to go back to Wellesley. Finally, after five years of contributing to the paper, she asked about a full-time staff position. The editors informed her that such a position was not available.

Reisig stopped writing for the *Village Voice* before she turned thirty. Concerning her experience at the *Village Voice*, she said, "I felt that most of my experience . . . was a very positive one. I loved writing for the *Voice*. I was able to write about subjects I cared about in the way I chose, and that was what mattered to me. It may mean I didn't earn much, but I knew that and made that choice consciously."[1]

She moved to Boston, where she found a job as a reporter for the underground newspaper the *Real Paper* before she worked at the *Washington Post*, for which she wrote about the women's liberation movement, including women's rights, among other topics.

Reisig returned to New York City and worked at *New York Newsday* as a features editor and an op-ed editor. She left the paper in the early 1980s and joined the faculty at Columbia University's Graduate School of Journalism, where she has been a successful instructor in the classroom.

In addition to teaching, she contributes articles and book reviews to various publications, including the *New Republic*, the *Nation*, and the *New York Times*.

SELECTED WORKS

Village Voice (reporter)
The Washington Post (reporter)
New York Newsday (editor)

NOTE

1. Ellen Frankfort, *The Voice: Life at the Village Voice* (New York: Morrow, 1976), 99.

REFERENCES

"Columbia University" website. www.journalism.columbia.edu (2008).
Frankfort, Ellen. *The Voice: Life at the Village Voice*. New York: Morrow, 1976.

Wilfrid Sheed (1930–)

WILFRID SHEED, A NOVELIST as well as an essayist, was born on December 27, 1930, in London, England. His parents, Maisie Ward Sheed and Frank Sheed, were Roman Catholic writers and publishers; indeed, they had founded Sheed and Ward, one of the most prestigious publishing houses of religious literature in the world, four years before their son was born. They opened a branch office in New York City in 1933.

When World War II began in Europe, Sheed moved with his parents and his sister, Rosemary, to the United States. They settled in Torresdale, Pennsylvania, a small town in which Sheed spent part of his youth. He was interested in sports; however, when he was stricken with poliomyelitis at fourteen, he acquired a taste for literature.

Sheed returned to England after his recuperation to attend the famous Benedictine preparatory school Downside Abbey, where he read works by Ernest Hemingway, Ring Lardner, E. M. Forster, P. G. Wodehouse, and James Thurber. Upon graduation, Sheed matriculated to Lincoln College, Oxford University, where he majored in history. He received his bachelor's degree in 1954. Within three years, he had earned a master's degree at Oxford. Part of his master's work, however, was completed at Columbia University in New York City.

Sheed then moved to Australia, where he lived with relatives. His desire to become a journalist was realized when he was hired by the Australian Broadcasting Company to report about sharks. This job did not last, and Sheed returned to the United States, where he wrote book and movie reviews as well as essays for various publications. He served as the film critic for the Catholic publication *Jubilee* from 1959 to 1961 and as its associate editor from 1959 to 1966. He served as drama critic as well as book review editor at *Commonweal*, another Catholic periodical, from 1964 to 1967. In 1967, he became a film critic at *Esquire*, a position that lasted two years. Although he contributed to the *New York Times Book Review* in 1971, his column "The Good Word" did not appear until later. Sheed also contributed numerous articles and essays to various other publications, including the *New York Review of Books*, *Saturday Evening Post*, *Life*, *Sports Illustrated*, *Commonweal*, and *Esquire*.

His first novel, *A Middle Class Education*, which appeared in 1960, was partly autobiographical. It was a satirical work about John Chote, who missed classes at Oxford University. Nonetheless, he received a scholarship to do graduate work at a university in the United States. Chote became involved with a woman and learned about life, but not through books. Finally, he returned to England, where he straightened out his life.

Sheed wrote other novels, some of which were about journalism and writers. Like his first, some were based on incidents in his life. *Office Politics: A Novel*, *Max Jamison: A Novel*, *People Will Always Be Kind*, and *Transatlantic Blues*, which were published in 1966, 1970, 1973, and 1978, respectively, received favorable reviews from critics.

His nonfiction brought him additional recognition. His book and film reviews as well as essays about sports, politics, politicians, and writers were published under the title *The Morning After: Selected Essays and Reviews* in 1971. Another collection of reviews and essays was published under the title *The Good Word and Other Words* in 1978. These collections were widely reviewed; many considered Sheed one of the best essayists writing for popular publications. In his review of *The Morning After*, Morris Freedman wrote, "The formal demands of his occasional writing . . . force a concentration on the epigram, the compact summation, the striking generalization. . . . To this highly professional skill Sheed . . . brings the restraint of common sense, balance and, most importantly, a sense of responsibility."[1]

Unlike some essayists, Sheed did not assert any particular ideology in his writing. Rather, he parodied and even revised conventional notions about his subjects. As John Leonard pointed out, "What's most characteristic about Sheed . . . is the care with which he chooses his subjects. He probes instead of devouring and understands without destroying."[2]

In *The Morning After*, Sheed recounted an incident that occurred while he was involved in the presidential campaign of Eugene McCarthy. Sheed recorded his own movements as well as his own thoughts as Robert Kennedy was shot and killed. Sheed became a participant in what he reported. He described in depth what he and others felt. He reported what individuals said. Accurate description, thoughts, and realistic dialogue made up the article, and the reader gained an insight into one terrible moment in man's uneven history as a result.

Essays in Disguise, another collection of informative essays that revealed Sheed's eye for detail and ear for language, was published in 1990. He employed an exciting prose style to present enlightening information about Frank Sinatra, Ernest Hemingway, John Updike, J. D. Salinger, the Mafia, and the Catholic Church, among other subjects. Sheed wrote other forms of nonfiction, including biographies of Muhammad Ali and Clare Booth Luce. He wrote an intimate account of his parents in *Frank & Maisie: A Memoir with Parents*, which was published in 1985.

In 1987, he wrote *The Boys of Winter*, a novel about a burned-out editor at a prestigious publishing house in New York City.

Sheed had grown fond of cricket when he lived in England. However, when he moved to the United States, this fondness was replaced by an interest in baseball. In *Baseball and Lesser Sports*, published in 1991, Sheed shared his affection with the reader, as he displayed his knowledge about baseball legends Connie Mack,

Joe DiMaggio, and Ted Williams, among others. He also discussed certain sportswriters and broadcasters, as well as the "lesser sports" of boxing and football.

Two years later, he wrote the witty, acerbic personal baseball memoir, *My Life as a Fan*, in which he affectionately recalled the Brooklyn Dodgers of the 1940s and 1950s. In 1995, he wrote *In Love with Daylight: A Memoir of Recovery*, a beautifully written book about his battle with cancer, alcohol, and prescription drugs.

In 2007, he examined the lives of composers and lyricists of American music in the book titled *House That George Built: With a Little Help from Irving, Cole, and a Crew of about Fifty*.

SELECTED WORKS

The Morning After: Selected Essays and Reviews (1971)
The Good Word and Other Words (1978)
Essays in Disguise (1990)

NOTES

1. Morris Freedman, "Mr. Sheed's Dryden," *New Republic*, October 2, 1971, 20.

2. Wilfrid Sheed, *The Morning After: Selected Essays and Reviews*, with a foreword by John Leonard (New York: Farrar, Straus & Giroux, 1971), xx.

REFERENCES

Sheed, Wilfrid. *Frank & Maisie: A Memoir with Parents*. New York: Simon & Schuster, 1985.
———. *My Life as a Fan*. New York: Simon & Schuster, 1993.
———. *In Love with Daylight: A Memoir of Recovery*. New York: Simon & Schuster, 1995.

Gail Sheehy (1937–)

Born on November 27, 1937, to Lillian Henion and Harold Merritt in Mamaroneck, New York, Gail Sheehy received her bachelor's degree from the University of Vermont in 1958. For the next two years, she worked as a home economist for the J. C. Penney Company. In 1961, she was hired as the fashion editor by the Rochester, New York, *Democrat and Chronicle*. This position lasted two years, until she moved to the *New York Herald Tribune*. For three years, until 1966, Sheehy wrote features on various subjects. This experience enabled her to move to *New York* magazine as a contributing editor in 1968. She remained at *New York* until 1977, when she left to write full-time.

Sheehy married Albert Sheehy in 1960; they divorced eight years later. In 1970, her first book, *Lovesounds*, was published. A novel, it concerned a husband and wife, their child, and a marriage that had grown stale—divorce was inevitable. Although the novel received some positive reviews, Sheehy turned to nonfiction, which she found easier to write. In 1971, *New York* published "Redpants," an article for which Sheehy interviewed numerous prostitutes. Redpants was a composite character based on a number of prostitutes. However, the reader was not made aware of this point, and, as a result, Sheehy was criticized by several journalists. The article and her subsequent book, *Hustling: Prostitution in Our Wide Open Society*, which appeared in 1973, utilized literary devices, includ-

174

ing careful description, scene-by-scene construction, and authentic dialogue, as well as the author's perspectives.

Sheehy also wrote several best-selling books that explored psychological as well as sociological issues. *Passages: Predictable Crises of Adult Life*, which was published in 1976, concerned the four major passages that people experience. *Pathfinders*, which followed in 1981, explored other areas or "paths" that would help people learn about themselves.

In 1986, she wrote *Spirit of Survival*, which was about her adopted daughter, Mohm, whose family was annihilated by the Pol Pot regime in Cambodia, and her years of witnessing countless murders. The book was insightful and passionate.

Two years later, she wrote *Character: America's Search for Leadership*, in which she focused on individuals who wanted to enter politics primarily to become president: Gary Hart, Albert Gore, Michael Dukakis, Jesse Jackson, Robert Dole, George Bush, and Ronald Reagan. In 1990, she wrote *The Man Who Changed the World: The Lives of Mikhail S. Gorbachev*, a perceptive biography that conveyed Gorbachev's ambition and self-assurance.

Sheehy examined the medical, psychological, and social aspects of menopause in *The Silent Passage: Menopause* in 1992. Sheehy claimed that the process spanned five to seven years and had three stages: perimenopause, menopause, and coalescence.

Her book *New Passages: Mapping Your Life across Time* was published in 1995 and explained how people could customize their life cycles. Three years later, she wrote *Understanding Men's Passages: Discovering the New Map of Men's Lives*, in which she examined the life stages and passages that men experience. Sheehy also dealt with problems that men faced, including baldness and retirement.

Sheehy, who had interviewed Hillary Rodham Clinton in 1992 for an article, wrote *Hillary's Choice*, which was published in 1999. Although much of what Sheehy presented had been reported by others, her biography offered something that few, if any, had—the psychological makeup of Clinton. Indeed, Sheehy explored Clinton's reasons for remaining with an unfaithful husband as well as her reasons for her personal aspirations.

Middletown, America: One Town's Passage from Trauma to Hope was published in 2003 and concerned numerous family members of those who had perished on September 11, 2001, when terrorists took control of four planes and subsequently killed nearly three thousand people by flying the jets into the World Trade Center in New York City, the Pentagon in Washington, D.C., and the ground near Shanksville, Pennsylvania.

In 2006, *Sex and the Seasoned Woman: Pursuing the Passionate Life* was published. In this book, Sheehy examined older women and their sexuality, including physical problems.

SELECTED WORKS

Hustling: Prostitution in Our Wide Open Society (1973)
Passages: Predictable Crises of Adult Life (1976)
Pathfinders (1981)
Spirit of Survival (1986)
The Silent Passage: Menopause (1992)
New Passages: Mapping Your Life across Time (1995)
Understanding Men's Passages: Discovering the New Map of Men's Lives (1998)
Middletown, America: One Town's Passage from Trauma to Hope (2003)
Sex and the Seasoned Woman: Pursuing the Passionate Life (2006)

REFERENCES

Bronson, Tammy J. "Gail Sheehy: Overview." *Contemporary Popular Writers.* Edited by Dave Mote. Detroit: St. James, 1997.
"Gail Sheehy." *Publisher's Weekly* 233, no. 20 (May 20, 1988), 65–66.
Schneider, Martin. "Exploring the 'New Novel.'" *Publisher's Weekly* 250, no. 32 (August 11, 2003), 270.

Richard Steele
(1672–1729)

BORN IN DUBLIN, IRELAND, in 1672, Richard Steele's father, an attorney, died four years later. Steele's mother died the following year. Henry Gascoigne, Steele's uncle, became his guardian.

Steele attended the Charterhouse School in London in 1684, where he met Joseph Addison. Both attended Oxford University. Addison, who studied Greek and Roman writers and published Latin compositions before graduation, was a more accomplished writer than Steele. Unlike Addison, Steele never graduated; he enlisted in the Guards. When he composed a poem on Queen Mary's death, which he dedicated to Lord Cutts, he was commissioned an ensign. He wrote several plays that were modestly successful, but he failed to make a comfortable living. He received a salary when he was appointed gazetteer in 1709. His expenses, however, exceeded his income.

In the years following, he frequently saw Addison and Jonathan Swift, both of whom contributed to *The Tatler*, which Steele published under the pseudonym Isaac Bickerstaff, a name he borrowed with permission from Swift's "Predictions for the year 1708, wherein the month and day of the month are set down, the persons named, and the great actions and events of next year particularly related, as they will come to pass. Written to prevent the people of England from being further imposed on by vulgar almanack-makers. By Isaac Bickerstaff, Esq."[1] The first issue was published

April 12, 1709. According to George Aitken, "The aim was to instruct the public what to think, after their reading, and there was to be something for the entertainment of the fair sex."[2]

The Tatler, a single folio sheet, appeared three times a week and cost a penny. Although initiated for the purpose of providing news (in his position as gazetteer, Steele knew what political activities were occurring), the need for these items died after the first eighty issues; rarely did Steele believe that some issue needed reporting.[3] As Aitken explained, "The subject of each article was to be indicated by the name of the coffee-house or other place from which it was supposed to come: 'All accounts of gallantry, pleasure, and entertainment shall be under the article of White's chocolate-house; Poetry, under that of Will's coffee-house; Learning, under the title of Grecian; Foreign and Domestic News you will have from Saint James's coffee-house; and what else I have to offer on any subject shall be dated from my own apartment.'"[4]

The Tatler belonged to Steele; it was his idea, and most of the material was written by him. When the publication began, Addison was living in Ireland; in fact, he was unaware that Steele published the paper until a statement he had made to Steele appeared in one of the issues. Only then did he occasionally submit contributions. According to Aitken, Steele wrote approximately 188 of the 271 papers, while Addison wrote 42; together they were responsible for 36.[5]

The first four issues were characteristic of the paper. The reader found an account of a gentleman at White's chocolate house who was saddened by a passing young lady; a notice of a benefit performance for Thomas Betterton; an account of the war with France; a declaration against John Partridge; a discussion on the morality of the stage; the benefit for Mrs. Bignell, which included a discourse on manners since a young man had attended the benefit intoxicated; a comparison of Chloe and Clarissa, or Mrs. Chetwine and Mrs. Hales, respectively; a satiric critique of the Italian opera *Pyrrhus and Demetrius*; and an allegorical article on Felicia, or Britain.[6]

According to Aitken, in addition to the disappearance of the news, *The Tatler*'s principal change "was the development of the sustained essay on morals or manners, and the less frequent indulgence in satire upon individual offenders, and in personal allusions in general."[7] Addison's interests probably were taken into consideration, since he and Steele occasionally worked together and were close friends.

Although *The Tatler* was read for its genial treatment of human follies and weaknesses such as pride, vanity, and impudence, Steele incorporated sharp attacks on gambling, dueling, brutality, and drinking. His various characters were alive. They brought the reader from the clubs to the coffeehouses. The reader saw the poets, the politicians, the Templars, and the merchants at the various coffeehouses. The reader saw Betterton, the plays, and the audience. The reader saw Powell's puppet show and the bear baiting and prize fights at Hockley-in-the-Hole. The reader experienced the Mall at St. James's or the Ring in Hyde Park. The reader visualized the fine ladies who shopped in Charles Lillie's, the perfumer, or in Mather's toy shop, or in Motteux's china warehouse. The reader saw the men who shopped in the stores in the New Exchange and their expressions. The reader saw the prominent clergymen in their respective churches and heard their messages on High and Low Church, Whig and Tory. The reader learned about the war with France, about the military leaders and their soldiers. The reader experienced the battles, including the glorious victories and the battered defeats.[8]

Steele lost his post as Gazetteer in October 1710, when the Whigs fell from power. *The Tatler* ceased publication in 1711.

Two years later, he started *The Guardian*, another paper. Like the previous one, *The Guardian* contained humor and satire. It featured Nestor Ironside and members of the Lizard family. Steele also criticized the government. When he was elected to Parliament later the same year, he turned the paper over to Addison. Steele wrote *The Importance of Dunkirk Considered*, a pamphlet that presented his views toward the Treaty of Utrecht, which he did not like. The Tories, who opposed Steele's views, responded. Jonathan Swift, for instance, wrote *The Importance of the Guardian Considered*, which attacked Steele. Steele stopped publishing *The Guardian*.

However, Steele published *The Englishman*, in which he announced his independence as a member of Parliament. To say the least, this riled the Tories, who examined every issue that Steele published.

When Steele published a pamphlet in which he discussed royal succession—specifically, the possibility that the Catholic Pretender might be introduced when the queen died—the Tories reacted. Swift wrote anonymously *The Publick Spirit of the Whigs* in 1714. Swift attempted to calm Steele and the Whigs' fears and referred to Steele's allegations as being seditious. Because Steele's name had appeared on his pamphlet and because Swift had brought up "sedition" in his anonymous pamphlet, the Tories voted against Steele in the House of Commons. Steele was expelled on March 18, 1714. However, within a year, when Queen Anne died, the Tories' power faded.

After *The Englishman* Steele published the paper *The Lover*, which concerned love. After forty issues, the paper ceased to exist. Although Steele published another paper, *The Reader*, it lasted only a few issues.

Steele not only returned to Parliament in 1715 but was knighted by King George I the same year. The Whigs encouraged Steele to publish another paper. *The Englishman* appeared anonymously later the same year. Steele did not necessarily agree with every idea or opinion the Whigs expressed, so he left his name out of the paper. The paper lasted thirty-eight issues.

Steele published a few additional papers, but these concerned the theater, for the most part, not necessarily politics. He also accused his old friend, Addison, of masquerading as a Whig, when Addison approved of the government's position in the Peerage Bill. Addison never forgave Steele before his death several years later.

Steele fathered an illegitimate daughter in the late 1600s and married Margaret Stretch, a widow, in 1705. Stretch died a year later. He married Mary Scurlock in 1707; she died in 1718. They had several children.

Steele retired in 1724. He died on September 1, 1729.

Selected Works

The Tatler (founder)
The Guardian (founder)
The Englishman (two different papers, founder)
The Lover (founder)
The Reader (founder)
Various political pamphlets

Notes

1. George A. Aitken, ed., *The Tatler* (New York: Hadley & Mathews, 1899), vii–x.
2. Aitken, ed., *The Life of Richard Steele*, xi.
3. Aitken, ed., *The Life of Richard Steele*.
4. Aitken, ed., *The Life of Richard Steele*, xii.
5. Aitken, ed., *The Life of Richard Steele*, xiv.
6. Aitken, ed., *The Life of Richard Steele*, 11–45.
7. Aitken, ed., *The Life of Richard Steele*, xix.
8. Aitken, ed., *The Life of Richard Steele*, xxiii–xxiv.

References

Aitken, George A. *The Life of Richard Steele*. 2 vols. London: Isbister, 1889.
Dammers, Richard H. *Richard Steele*. Boston: Twayne, 1982.
Winton, Calhoun. *Captain Steele*. Baltimore: Johns Hopkins University Press, 1964.

Gloria Steinem (1934-)

FEMINIST, ACTIVIST, COLUMNIST, WRITER, and editor, Gloria Steinem was born on March 25, 1934, in Toledo, Ohio. Her father and mother divorced before she reached adolescence, but her mother, who had formerly worked as a reporter before she married, obtained a similar position in Toledo and was able to support Gloria and herself.

Steinem moved to Washington, D.C., to live with her older sister. When she completed her secondary education, her mother made the financial arrangements so she could attend Smith College. Steinem proved to be an excellent student and consequently received a scholarship. When she graduated in 1956, she received a fellowship to travel and study at the University of Delhi and the University of Calcutta. Upon her return to the United States, she worked as the director of the Independent Research Service in Cambridge, Massachusetts, and then as a writer for *Esquire* in New York City, to which she contributed "The Moral Disarmament of Betty Coed" and "Student Prince." Although she remained with the magazine for a few years, she moved to *Show* in 1963. Perhaps her most important contribution to this magazine was "A Bunny Tale," which was based on her experience as a bunny in a Playboy Club. Articles about her humorous exposé of Hugh Hefner's dream turned reality appeared in news magazines, and Steinem's career as a journalist was secure. Her byline was seen in such publications as

Life, *Vogue*, *McCall's*, *Cosmopolitan*, and *Glamour*, and she wrote for the NBC series "That Was the Week That Was."

Steinem, who became a celebrity for what she wrote and for what she advocated for women, wrote features on James Baldwin, Julie Andrews, Jackie Kennedy, Barbra Streisand, Truman Capote, Michael Caine, Dame Margot Fonteyn, and Lee Bouvier, and on topics such as women and power, Englishmen and their opinions of American women, fashion, popular culture, Lefrak City, and women's liberation, among others.

In each interview she conducted, Steinem captured intelligently the scene, the personality, and especially the mannerisms and the moods. Some of her profiles included colorful descriptive passages about the person interviewed. Some of these passages allowed the personalities to present themselves in their own words. For most of the interviews, she included background information, information that she deemed beneficial to the reader. Her advocating articles logically explored issues that concerned her as a woman. Usually she presented the facts and then her beliefs as to what should be done to correct the problems. If she believed that the problems could be better illustrated with description or anecdotes, she would use either or both.

In 1968, Steinem was hired by Clay Felker to write for his newly resurrected *New York* magazine. Steinem wrote numerous advocacy articles about women, marriages, and politics. She attacked Eugene McCarthy and Richard Nixon, she supported Norman Mailer's and Jimmy Breslin's political aspirations, and she wrote and spoke with vengeance for numerous minority groups. Her *New York* column "The City Politic" was never subtle as long as there was a cause of some kind.

In the late 1960s, Steinem became involved in the feminist movement, and in 1972, she became editor of *Ms.*, a magazine she cofounded for the liberated woman. *Ms.* promoted the ideas of Steinem and other feminists. By the mid-1970s, the magazine had attracted half a million readers.

Steinem was one of the commissioners appointed by President Jimmy Carter to the National Committee on the Observance of International Women's Year in 1977. She was awarded a Woodrow

Wilson Scholarship to study feminism at the Woodrow Wilson International Center for Scholars the same year.

During the 1980s, Steinem continued editing *Ms.*, as well as supporting various women's organizations. A collection of her essays, articles, and diary entries was published in 1983 under the title *Outrageous Acts and Everyday Rebellions*. The collection included "I Was a Playboy Bunny"; "Ruth's Song," which concerned her mother; and articles on several famous women. The collection contained examples of advocacy journalism as well as literary journalism.

In 1986, Steinem's insightful biography of Marilyn Monroe was published. Titled *Marilyn: Norma Jean*, the book was more realistic than other biographies of Monroe in the sense that it focused on her personality and entire life, not just the years in Hollywood. Steinem revealed a warm human being who had childlike qualities. Unfortunately, the child was trapped in a woman's body.

One year later, *Ms.* was sold to a large Australian communications conglomerate. Steinem was retained as an editor. The magazine was sold again, and Steinem remained as editor. In 1988, she became a consulting editor to the magazine and an editorial consultant to Random House, a publishing firm.

In 1992, Steinem wrote *Revolution from Within: A Book of Self-Esteem*, which was a self-help book that attempted to inform readers how to boost their self-esteem. Steinem used other sources, including Margaret Mead and Chief Seattle, as well as her own life, for inspiration. She offered literature, nature, art, meditation, and connectedness as means of finding and exploring the self. In her review of the book for *Newsweek*, Laura Shapiro wrote, "If anything distinguishes 'Revolution from Within' from dozens of other contributions to the genre, it's Steinem's feminist politics, which are prominent or at least discernible throughout."[1]

Moving beyond Words, a book of six essays, three of which had appeared in magazines, was published in 1994. The essays included "What If *Freud* Were *Phyllis*?" in which Steinem claimed that Freud's theories had been based on the assumption of male superiority. In "Sex, Lies and Advertising," she examined the advertising business as it applied to magazines. In "The Strongest Woman in the World," Steinem described the female bodybuilder Bev Francis.

She wrote about wealthy women who had lost control of their trust funds in "The Masculinization of Wealth." In "Revolving Economics," she detailed how worldwide census and accounting practices undervalued women's labor; in "Doing Sixty," Steinem explored her life at sixty.

In 2006, she expanded her essay "Doing Sixty," which had appeared in *Moving beyond Words*, and added "Seventy" for the book *Doing Sixty & Seventy*.

SELECTED WORKS

Ms. (cofounder and editor)
Outrageous Acts and Everyday Rebellions (1983)
Revolution from Within: A Book of Self-Esteem (1992)
Moving beyond Words (1994)

NOTE

1. Laura Shapiro, "Little Gloria, Happy at Last," *Newsweek*, January 13, 1992, 64.

REFERENCES

Heilbrun, Carolyn. *The Education of a Woman: The Life of Gloria Steinem*. New York: Dial, 1995.

Lazo, Caroline Evensen. *Gloria Steinem: Feminist Extraordinaire*. Minneapolis, Minn.: Lerner, 1998.

Stern, Sydney Ladensohn. *Gloria Steinem: Her Passions, Politics, and Mystique*. New York: Carol, 1997.

Simeon Strunsky
(1879–1948)

SIMEON STRUNSKY WAS BORN TO Pearl and Isadore Strunsky in Vitebsk, Russia, in 1879, and was brought to New York City when he was seven. He lived with his brothers, sisters, and parents on the Lower East Side. He received Pulitzer scholarships to Columbia's Horace Mann School and to Columbia College (Columbia University); he graduated from the latter in 1900.

Strunsky worked for the *New International Encyclopedia* from 1900 to 1906. He married Rebecca Slobodkin in 1905. Although they had a son, she died a year later. Strunsky then joined the staff of Oswald Garrison Villard's *New York Evening Post*, where he wrote numerous editorials and humorous essays on current events. He married Manya Gordon in 1910, and they eventually had a daughter.

In 1912, his essays concerning Theodore Roosevelt's efforts to regain the White House received considerable recognition. Strunsky's perceptiveness was evident, for even Roosevelt enjoyed reading the essays. His style, which was evidently influenced by such writers as William Hazlitt and G. K. Chesterton, was extremely witty.

In addition to writing for the *Post*, Strunsky contributed to Villard's *Nation* and the *Atlantic Monthly*. His essays were collected and published under the titles *The Patient Observer and His Friends*, in 1911, and *Belshazzar Court; or, Village Life in New York*

City, in 1914. In 1918, he published his first novel, *Prof. Latimer's Progress*, which concerned several characters who lived and worked in New York City. However, his essays, although mild compared to other forms of journalism at the time, became his dominant form of expression. For instance, when World War I began, Strunsky advocated Allied support and laissez-faire economics, satirized the Germans, and opposed Bolshevism. In fact, his satire of the Germans was republished under the title *Little Journeys towards Paris*, which was published in 1918. At the end of the war, he reported on the Paris Peace Conference as well as the Washington Disarmament Conference.

In 1920, Strunsky became chief editorial writer of the *New York Evening Post*. However, four years later, when Thomas W. Lamont, the owner, sold the paper to Cyrus H. K. Curtis, Strunsky joined the *New York Times*, for which he wrote editorials and the weekly column "About Books—More or Less." Cyrus H. K. Curtis was, Strunsky believed, too conservative about editorial policies.

In 1932, Strunsky was given the responsibility of writing "Topics of the Times," a daily column on the editorial page. Immediately, Strunsky incorporated his liberal political beliefs; he learned, however, that a column contained little space for his ideas. Consequently, *The Living Tradition*, which concerned American values, was published in 1939, followed by *No Mean City*, which concerned New York City, five years later. His last book, *Two Came to Town*, which was also about New York City, was published in 1947.

Strunsky, an advocate for the American way of life, held onto his liberal beliefs until the end. His writing—much of it informal, less vehement perhaps than that of the earlier advocating journalists—awakened the public and the politicians to his way of thinking.

He died of cancer in February 1948.

SELECTED WORKS

The Patient Observer and His Friends (1911)
Belshazzar Court; or, Village Life in New York City (1914)

REFERENCES

"Simeon Strunsky of the *Times* Dies: Author of Topics Column for 15 Years Once Editor of *Post*—Wrote Many Books." *New York Times,* February 6, 1948, 23.
Strunsky, Simeon. *Simeon Strunsky's America: "Topics of the Times,"* 1933–1947. Comp. Harold Phelps Stokes. New York: N.p., 1956.

Harvey Swados
(1920-1972)

HARVEY SWADOS WAS BETTER KNOWN as a novelist perhaps than as a critical essayist who promoted socialism for the working man, especially the blue-collar worker, but he was undoubtedly an advocate for the faceless citizen.

Born to Rebecca and Aaron Swados in Buffalo on October 28, 1920, Swados joined the Young Communist League while in high school. He matriculated to the University of Michigan, where he accepted Trotskyism. He graduated in 1940 and returned to Buffalo, where he worked in several factories for a few years while he tried to establish himself as a writer. Although he married Billie Aronson, they soon separated and eventually divorced. Swados moved to New York City.

From 1942 to 1945, he served as a radio operator in the U.S. Merchant Marine, sailing the Atlantic as well as the Pacific. When he returned to the States, he settled in New York City, where he wrote *The Unknown Constellations*, a novel that no publisher accepted.

In 1946, he married Bette Beller. They moved to Valley Cottage, New York, and started a family. Swados worked at several part-time jobs for the next several years and wrote short stories and essays for various publications, including *Esquire*, *Partisan Review*, the *Saturday Evening Post*, and the *Nation*. In 1955, his novel *Out Went the Candle* was published. The novel concerned a businessman who

REFERENCES

Fried, Joseph P. "Harvey Swados, Novelist, Dies; Wrote Widely on Social Scene." *New York Times*, December 12, 1972, 52.

Moore, Harry T., ed. *Contemporary American Novelists*. Carbondale: Southern Illinois University Press, 1964.

Swados, Harvey. *The Unknown Constellations*. Foreword and introduction by Neil D. Isaacs. Urbana: University of Illinois Press, 1995.

Wald, Alan M. *The New York Intellectuals: The Rise and Decline of the Anti-Stalinist Left from the 1930s to the 1980s*. Chapel Hill: University of North Carolina Press, 1987.

Temple's personal library and wrote very poor eulogistic poems that imitated the style of Abraham Cowley. Swift enjoyed working for Temple, but his health deteriorated because of the damp climate.

In 1690, Swift returned to Ireland, but his health did not improve. In less than a year, he was back at Moor Park. While he worked for Temple, he completed his master's degree at Oxford University. In 1693, one of his first essays was published. Titled *An Answer to a Scurrilous Pamphlet, Lately Printed, Intituled, a Letter from Monsieur De Cros*, the essay defended Temple against attacks that had been made against him when he was a diplomat for Charles II. The anonymous essay appeared in pamphlet form and was filled with sarcasm.

In 1694, Swift was ordained into the Church of Ireland and was assigned to Northern Ireland, one of the poorest areas, which he disliked. Indeed, within two years he was back at Moor Park, where he remained until 1699, the year Temple died.

While he was living and working at Moor Park, Swift wrote *A Tale of a Tub. Written for the Universal Improvement of Mankind. Diu multumque desideratum. To Which Is Added, an Account of a Battel between the Antient and Modern Books in St. James's Library.* In this work, he defended Temple and his assumption that the learning of the ancients was superior to that of the moderns against Richard Bentley, who had attacked Temple and his literary notion. The essay was published anonymously in 1704. Swift did not necessarily agree with Temple; he was merely offended by Bentley's tone, which had sounded too personal. Swift redefined *ancient* and *modern* and had a battle between books in a library, which represented each term. Through allegories, Swift satirized values as well as religion, preferring the Church of England and Church of Ireland over Catholicism and Protestantism.

Swift became chaplain to Charles, earl of Berkeley, in Ireland. He also became vicar of Laracor and was given the prebend of Dunlavin in St. Patrick's Cathedral in Dublin. This position encouraged him to become involved in religious and political affairs in England. In 1701, for instance, he returned to England and learned that four Whig ministers might be impeached because they had been charged with arranging treaties without consulting or informing

Parliament. Swift, who considered himself a Whig, criticized the impeachment of the four Whig ministers in *A Discourse of the Contests and Dissensions between the Nobles and the Commons in Athens and Rome, with the Consequences They Had upon Both Those States*, which was published the same year.

Swift returned to Ireland in 1702 and earned the doctor of divinity degree from Trinity College later that year. He devoted most of his time to his parish and to St. Patrick's Cathedral.

In 1707, he returned to England as a representative of the Church of Ireland, but he was more productive as a writer than as a negotiator for funds. His poetry and essays appeared in *The Tatler*, which was published by Richard Steele.

At this time, Swift realized that he differed with the Whigs. The Whigs supported Protestant dissenters who did not support the Test Act; Swift was loyal to the Church of England and consequently supported the act. Therefore, his writing attacked the dissenters and their views toward the act. He also called for the queen to appoint virtuous men to positions of power.

Swift returned to Ireland in 1709. The Whigs, who had taken control of Parliament in 1708, were ousted in 1710, and the political climate in England changed drastically when Robert Harley's ministry came to power. Swift returned to England, and Harley paid the "First Fruits and Twentieth Parts"—fees that had been paid by the clergy in Ireland to the British Crown—to Swift. Harley, who favored a coalition government, persuaded Swift to write on behalf of the new Tory government. Swift, who now referred to himself as an "Old Whig," was like Daniel Defoe in that he supported Harley's "initially moderate but eventually extremist Tory ministry."[1]

The Tory ministry published the *Examiner*, a weekly paper, in 1710. Harley asked Swift to serve as writer and editor. Swift captured the public's attention almost immediately and was invited to cabinet meetings, formal dinners, and gala affairs at Windsor. Yet his essays were conservative, for the most part, in that he defended certain actions of the ministry and advocated peace. He attacked John Churchill, duke of Marlborough, among others, claiming that he was corrupt and an enemy of England. Like *The Tatler* and later *The Spectator*, the *Examiner* published letters addressed to the editor, responses from the editor, and essays that contained fables and other literary devices to enhance the topic being discussed. Swift's writing was straightforward yet filled with sarcasm. He stopped editing the paper in 1711 and returned to writing political propaganda in pamphlet form, such as the best-selling *The Conduct of the Allies, and of the Late Ministry, in Beginning and Carrying on the Present War*. This pamphlet summarized the ministry's perspective toward the war with France and then presented strong arguments for peace. Swift also charged that the Whigs had prolonged the War of the Spanish Succession primarily for selfish reasons. The writing was terse and clear, and the arguments were sound. The reader easily understood the author's points and subsequently reacted to those points.

Swift observed the feuding between Harley and Henry St. John, who was made Viscount Bolingbroke in 1712 and called for a unilateral treaty with France. Harley desired that the Dutch be included; eventually, his desires were fulfilled when the Treaty of Utrecht was signed in 1713.

The same year, Swift was made dean of St. Patrick's Cathedral in Dublin. He returned to England, however, where he attempted to ease the tension between Harley and St. John. Unfortunately, it was too late. Swift wrote the controversial *The Publick Spirit of the Whigs: Set Forth in Their Generous Encouragement of the Author of the Crisis: With Some Observations on the Seasonableness, Candor, Erudition, and Style of That Treatise* and faced possible prosecution because the Tories no longer reigned. The queen had died in 1714; George I and the Whig ministry had assumed power. Swift immediately left England for Ireland, where he continued as dean of St. Patrick's Cathedral. He eventually wrote about the exploitation and enslavement of Ireland by England as well as the friction between the various political and religious factions that made up Irish society.

Swift favored restrictions on Catholics and dissenters, but he opposed economic restrictions on Ireland by England. He expressed these views in *A Proposal for the Universal Use of Irish Manufacture, in Cloaths and Furniture of Houses, etc., Uterly Rejecting and Renouncing Every Thing Wearable That Comes from England*, which was published in 1720. In a series of letters, he argued against using coins manufactured by William Wood, who had been authorized by England to coin a hundred thousand pounds worth of Irish coins. Swift claimed that the coins contained too little copper and would glut the market, thus reducing the value of money. Wood's authorization was withdrawn in 1725.

Although Swift's satiric *Travels into Several Remote Nations of the World. In Four Parts. By Lemuel Gulliver, First a Surgeon, and Then a Captain of several Ships* was published in 1726, he continued to write political essays. In 1729, for instance, his *A Modest Proposal for Preventing the Children of Poor People from Being a Burthen to Their Parents, or the Country, and for Making Them Beneficial to the Publick* was published. In this attack on England's treatment of the Irish people, Swift proposed that children of poor inhabitants of Ireland should be sold to the wealthy for food. He compared the poor to cattle and provided images of slaughtering and cooking the children. Swift used analogies, metaphors, and other literary devices to strengthen his arguments. The pamphlet, which was easily understood, was controversial because of its subject matter.

Swift wrote an occasional political essay and numerous poems during the next several years. After 1734, however, his interest in writing declined. Ill health and forgetful memory bothered him until his death in 1745. He was seventy-seven.

Swift's political essays were early examples of advocacy journalism. As an advocate of political and religious thought, he persuaded multitudes of people, including clergy and representatives of governments, to accept his particular positions.

SELECTED WORKS

An Answer to a Scurrilous Pamphlet, Lately Printed, Intituled, a Letter from Monsieur De Cros (1693)
A Tale of a Tub. Written for the Universal Improvement of Mankind. Diu multumque desideratum. To Which Is Added, an Account of a Battel between the Antient and Modern Books in St. James's Library (1704)

A Discourse of the Contests and Dissensions between the Nobles and the Commons in Athens and Rome, with the Consequences They Had upon Both Those States (1710)

The Conduct of the Allies, and of the Late Ministry, in Beginning and Carrying on the Present War (1712)

The Publick Spirit of the Whigs: Set Forth in Their Generous Encouragement of the Author of the Crisis: With Some Observations on the Seasonableness, Candor, Erudition, and Style of That Treatise (1714)

A Prospect for the Universal Use of Irish Manufacture, in Cloaths and Furniture of Houses, etc., Uterly Rejecting and Renouncing Every Thing Wearable That Comes from England (1720)

A Modest Proposal for Preventing the Children of Poor People from Being a Burthen to Their Parents, or the Country, and for Making Them Beneficial to the Publick (1729)

NOTE

1. Laura Ann Curtis, ed., *The Versatile Defoe* (Totowa, N.J.: Rowman & Littlefield, 1979), 10.

REFERENCES

Ehrenpreis, Irvin. *Swift: The Man, His Works, and the Age.* 3 vols. Cambridge, Mass.: Harvard University Press, 1962–1983.

Nokes, David. *Jonathan Swift, a Hypocrite Reversed: A Critical Biography.* Oxford: Oxford University Press, 1985.

Quintana, Ricardo. *The Mind and Art of Jonathan Swift.* Oxford: Oxford University Press, 1936.

Voight, Milton. *Swift and the Twentieth Century.* Detroit: Wayne State University Press, 1964.

Gore Vidal (1925–)

EUGENE LUTHER VIDAL, OR GORE VIDAL, was born on October 3, 1925, at the United States Military Academy in West Point, New York, where his father was an instructor in aeronautics. Vidal's grandfather, Thomas Pryor Gore, was Oklahoma's first senator. Vidal stayed with his grandfather in Washington, D.C., primarily to assist him, until his parents divorced in 1935. He learned about history and politics from reading books on the subjects to his grandfather, who was blind, as well as from leading his grandfather around the nation's capital. He attended St. Alban's School and then the Los Alamos School in New Mexico for a year. He completed his high school education at the prestigious Phillips Exeter Academy, where, in addition to writing for the academy's *Review*, he organized a student group that opposed America's involvement in World War II. His political philosophy had been molded by his grandfather's isolationist beliefs.

When Vidal graduated in 1943, he intended to enroll at Harvard. He enlisted, however, in the U.S. Army Reserve Corps and served on a transport ship in the Aleutians. Vidal read during his off-duty hours and wrote the novel *Williwaw*, which was published in 1946. The novel concerned the conflicts between crew members on board a military craft.

Vidal was released from service in 1946 and obtained a position editing books at E. P. Dutton, a publishing company in New York

City. Within six months, he left Dutton and moved to Antigua, Guatemala, believing he could earn his living from writing novels. *In a Yellow Wood*, which he had completed before he left New York City, appeared in 1947, to mostly favorable reviews. The novel depicts a veteran of World War II who has to adjust to civilian life. *The City and the Pillar: A Novel* explores one character's realization that he is a homosexual. To say the least, the book was attacked by certain critics for its unusual subject matter when it was published in 1948.

Vidal, who contracted hepatitis in 1947, returned to the United States for a while and then toured Europe, traveling through North Africa as well as Italy. After about two years, he returned to the United States.

Over the next several years, he wrote *The Season of Comfort*, which was published in 1949 and which was a slightly disguised autobiography of his early years; *A Search for the King: A Twelfth-Century Legend*, which was published in 1950 and described the search of Blondel de Neel for Richard the Lion-Hearted; *Dark Green, Bright Red*, which was published in 1950 and depicted the various exploits of an American mercenary soldier; *The Judgment of Paris*, which was published in 1952 and concerned an American who wandered through Europe; and *Messiah*, which was published in 1954 and focused on a new religion. These novels were dismissed by many critics, and it was evident that his novels were not going to sell. Vidal's financial resources dwindled.

Vidal wrote teleplays for several television programs. Later, he moved to Hollywood and wrote screenplays for Metro-Goldwyn-Mayer. Vidal's intention was to earn enough money in a relatively brief period so he could return to writing novels. Toward the end of the decade, however, he wrote for the stage. His first success was an adaptation of his *Visit to a Small Planet*, which had appeared on television in 1955. *The Best Man*, a satire about American politics, followed in 1960. He wrote other plays, but none were as successful as these.

By the early 1960s, Vidal had returned to the novel. *Julian: A Novel* was published in 1964 and concerned Flavius Claudius Julianus, the Roman emperor who attempted to restore paganism.

Washington, D.C.: A Novel, the first novel in his series about American history and politics, was published in 1967. *Burr: A Novel* followed in 1973 and was enjoyed by critics. The book *1876: A Novel*, which was published in 1976, was criticized by some reviewers for not having a major character to carry the plot.

Vidal also wrote the controversial satire *Myra Breckinridge*, which focused on transsexuality and American culture. Published in 1968, the novel was followed by *Myron: A Novel* in 1974, which concerned the further exploits of Myra. The critics panned the latter because the novel's situations were too repetitive.

Vidal penned other historical and political novels, including *Creation*, which was published in 1981, *Lincoln: A Novel*, which was published in 1984, *Empire: A Novel*, which was published in 1987, *Hollywood: A Novel of America in the 1920s*, which was published in 1990, and *The Golden Age: A Novel*, which was published in 2000.

He also wrote numerous advocating essays for several publications throughout the 1950s, 1960s, 1970s, 1980s, and 1990s. These essays, which concerned politics, Broadway literature, public television, writers, pornography, sex, flying, and himself, were collected in several books, including *Rocking the Boat*, which was published in 1962; *Sex, Death, and Money*, which was published in 1968; *Reflections upon a Sinking Ship*, which was published in 1969; *Matters of Fact and of Fiction: Essays, 1973–1976*, which was published in 1977; *The Second American Revolution and Other Essays (1976–1982)*, which was published in 1982; *At Home: Essays, 1982–1988*, which was published in 1988; *A View from the Diner's Club: Essays, 1987–1991*, which was published in 1991; and *The Decline and Fall of the American Empire*, which was published in 1992, among others. Other collections contained some of his best essays. These included *Homage to Daniel Shays: Collected Essays, 1952–1972*, which was published in 1972, and *United States: Essays, 1952–1992*, which was published in 1993.

Regarding Vidal's essays, Robert Graalman wrote, "Vidal argues just as emphatically for his beliefs as he does to reject a political tag. He can be an articulate and vigorous commentator against, for example, such a topic as the horrors of television advertising, for

something as grand as governmental responsibility, and most forc-
ibly for a more humane, realistic, and finally liberating attitude on
the subject of sexuality in Western civilization."[1]

Vidal's essays contained personal references to others as well
as allusions to historical events and figures. Many contained clips
from his past. In several essays about politics, one theme was ever
present—that the United States was controlled by a few power
brokers and corporations such as the Chase Manhattan Bank and
CBS. As Robert E. Kiernan pointed out, "Vidal is . . . a vocal critic
of the American establishment."[2] In summarizing his assessment
of Vidal's essays, Kiernan wrote, "The essays, like the novels, are a
banquet of canapés. They may leave one hungry for logical fair play,
as the novels leave one hungry for plot, but the canapés are so tasty
withal that more conventional fare seems unflavored."[3]

In 2001, *The Last Empire: Essays, 1992–2000* was published.
This collection contained commentary about literature and politics,
among other topics, and was favorably reviewed by critics. In 2002,
Vidal published *Dreaming War: Blood for Oil and the Cheney-Bush
Junta* and *Perpetual War for Perpetual Peace: How We Got to Be So
Hated*. In these books, Vidal's essays focused on the United States
after the terrorist attacks of September 11, 2001. Indeed, in the
first book, he drew parallels between the terrorist attacks and the
attack on Pearl Harbor and claimed that Bush, just like Roosevelt,
knew beforehand that the attacks would occur and subsequently
used the attacks for political purposes, especially in the Middle
East. Vidal also examined the Oklahoma City bombing, which, in
his opinion, was justified, as well as the government's assaults on
Ruby Ridge and Waco. In 2004, *Imperial America: Reflections on
the United States of Amnesia* was published. The essays in this book
criticized the Bush administration and its imperialistic policies.

Vidal wrote about his own life in 1992, in *The Screening of History*. Indeed, the book contained reminiscences of his childhood
and early manhood. These reminiscences were mixed with the
films that he saw when he was young. An unusual autobiography
because of this technique, it nonetheless provided another side to
the author. He examined his own life again in *Palimpsest: A Memoir*, which was published in 1995. The book covered the first four

decades, including the years he worked in Hollywood, the years he wrote plays, and the years he ran for political office. He continued his story in *Point to Point Navigation: A Memoir*, which was published in 2006. To be specific, he focused on the years from the mid-1960s to the early 2000s, writing about his relationships and experiences. The book is filled with stories about Vidal and other famous people. The book is also filled with Vidal's thoughts about the country and the world.

SELECTED WORKS

Rocking the Boat (1962)
Sex, Death, and Money (1968)
Reflections upon a Sinking Ship (1969)
Homage to Daniel Shays: Collected Essays, 1952–1972 (1972)
Matters of Fact and of Fiction: Essays, 1973–1976 (1977)
The Second American Revolution and Other Essays (1976–1982) (1982)
Armageddon? Essays, 1983–1987 (1987)
At Home: Essays, 1982–1988 (1988)
A View from the Diner's Club: Essays, 1987–1991 (1991)
The Decline and Fall of the American Empire (1992)
United States: Essays, 1952–1992 (1993)
The Last Empire: Essays, 1992–2000 (2001)
Dreaming War: Blood for Oil and the Cheney-Bush Junta (2002)
Perpetual War for Perpetual Peace: How We Got to Be So Hated (2002)
Imperial America: Reflections on the United States of Amnesia (2004)

NOTES

1. Robert Graalman, "Gore Vidal (3 October 1925–)," in *American Novelists since World War II: Second Series*, ed. James E. Kibler Jr. (Detroit: Gale Research, 1980), 346.

2. Robert F. Kiernan, *Gore Vidal* (New York: Ungar, 1982), 111.

3. Kiernan, *Gore Vidal*, 117.

REFERENCES

Dick, Bernard F. *The Apostate Angel: A Critical Study of Gore Vidal*. New York: Random House, 1974.

Kaplan, Fred. *Gore Vidal: A Biography*. New York: Doubleday, 1999.

Kiernan, Robert F. *Gore Vidal*. New York: Ungar, 1982.

Vidal, Gore. *Palimpsest: A Memoir*. New York: Random House, 1995.

———. *Point to Point Navigation: A Memoir*. New York: Doubleday, 2006.

White, Ray Lewis. *Gore Vidal*. New York: Twayne, 1968.

Nicholas von Hoffman
(1929–)

NICHOLAS VON HOFFMAN WAS BORN to Anna and Carl von Hoffman on October 16, 1929, in New York City, where he was educated at the Fordham Prep School. He entered journalism in the 1960s, after he had served as an associate director of the Industrial Areas Foundation and as Saul Alinsky's chief organizer of the Woodlawn Organization, which was founded to serve the needs of Chicago's South Side African American community.

In 1963, von Hoffman became a staff member of the *Chicago Daily News*, for which he covered the civil rights movement, including the movement called "Freedom Summer" in Mississippi. His revelations were ultimately collected in the diary-like *Mississippi Notebook*, which was published in 1964. He also wrote interpretative stories about American universities and the students who attended the various campuses. His book *The Multiversity: A Personal Report on What Happens to Today's Students at American Universities*, which was published in 1966, explored the same issues.

In 1966, von Hoffman joined the staff of the *Washington Post*, where, in addition to writing a column several times a week, he wrote stories on student riots, hippies, the Chicago Democratic convention, and Watergate. According to Benjamin Bradlee, former editor of the *Washington Post*, "von Hoffman's dispatches as written were landmarks in the early, timid years of the new journalism:

personal, pertinent, articulate, vital glimpses of man trying to make it in a more and more complicated world."[1]

Von Hoffman's book *We Are the People Our Parents Warned Us Against*, which told through the characters' own words what life in San Francisco's Haight-Ashbury district was like, was published in 1968.

A collection of von Hoffman's columns for the *Washington Post* appeared under the title *Left at the Post* in 1970. His columns were powerful. Indeed, what von Hoffman wrote "produced more angry letters to the editor than the work of any other single reporter" in the newspaper's history, according to Chalmers M. Roberts.[2]

Von Hoffman broadened his interests in the 1970s, when he debated James J. Kirkpatrick on CBS's *60 Minutes* and contributed numerous articles to such periodicals as the *Progressive, Harper's Bazaar, New Times,* and *Esquire*. Although he left the *Washington Post* in 1976, he became the Washington correspondent for the London-based *Spectator* magazine the same year. He also continued to write articles as well as books. For instance, his critical examination of politics in America, *Make-Believe Presidents: Illusions of Power from McKinley to Carter,* appeared in 1978.

In 1984, von Hoffman wrote the critically acclaimed novel *Organized Crimes,* which concerned the Chicago underworld of the 1930s. He had not written a novel since the 1960s.

Four years later von Hoffman returned to nonfiction with a biography titled *Citizen Cohn* that examined the controversial lawyer's social environment. He began with Roy Cohn's death from AIDS and then presented in chronological order almost every villainous deed that Cohn committed. Von Hoffman examined Cohn's possessive mother, who had despised her husband and had had a commanding effect on her son. Cohn, according to von Hoffman, was a closet homosexual until his mother died; then his affairs became well known. Von Hoffman also discussed Cohn's ongoing battles with the IRS and the New York State Bar Association. The book, which contained numerous quotes from Cohn's friends and enemies, revealed that Cohn was merely interested in law because it had provided the means to a particular end. The book was praised by critics for its coverage but not necessarily for its depth.

In 1992, von Hoffman wrote *Capitalist Fools: Tales of American Business, from Carnegie to Forbes to the Milken Gang*, which was part biography and part history. Von Hoffman critically examined Malcolm Forbes and the men he profiled in his magazine, claiming that the executives had profited from buyouts and stock option plans while their businesses declined. Although sarcasm appeared throughout the narrative, von Hoffman honored certain heroes such as B. C. Forbes, Malcolm's father who had founded *Forbes* magazine; Daniel McCallum, who had operated the railroads during the Civil War; and John Patterson, the maverick tyrant who had been responsible for building the National Cash Register company. According to von Hoffman, the number of executives who can be classified as heroes has decreased:

> These sorts of people are far more infrequent now. There are some marvelous people who have done wonderful things—I mention a few in the book—but the culture has changed enormously. One of the themes of this book is that in the process of creating itself, business changed the culture that made it—it ate its young. The commercial parts of our society use pleasure ubiquitously to sell merchandise and teach people to become obsessive pleasure lovers: "I won't do it unless it's fun; I don't like that teacher because he or she is not entertaining." Well, some things are arduous and they do hurt.[3]

In 2004, von Hoffman wrote the insightful *Hoax: Why Americans Are Suckered by White House Lies*, which analyzed the foreign policy of the Bush administration as well as its strategy for persuading the public to support the invasion of Iraq. To say the least, von Hoffman's criticism of the Bush administration did not sit well with Bush supporters.

One of von Hoffman's columns illustrated his advocating journalistic style. Opinionated, stereotypical, the column seemed to be against fat African American women who received welfare—that is, until the last three sentences. In these sentences, von Hoffman presented the women's arguments and then through the use of a metaphor illustrated their predicament. The metaphor suggested that immediate measures should be implemented to correct the problem discussed.

Selected Works

Mississippi Notebook (1964)
We Are the People Our Parents Warned Us Against (1968)
Left at the Post (1970)
Make-Believe Presidents: Illusions of Power from McKinley to Carter (1978)
Capitalist Fools: Tales of American Business, from Carnegie to Forbes to the Milken Gang (1992)
Hoax: Why Americans Are Suckered by White House Lies (2004)

Notes

1. Nicholas von Hoffman, *Left at the Post* (Chicago: Quadrangle Books, 1970), 8.
2. Chalmers M. Roberts, "Hoffman, Nicholas von," *Contemporary Authors*, vol. 81–84, ed. Francis Carol Locher (Detroit: Gale Research, 1979), 586.
3. Wendy Smith, "PW Interviews Nicholas von Hoffman," *Publishers Weekly*, September 21, 1992, 72.

References

Roberts, Chalmers M. *The Washington Post: The First 100 Years*. Boston: Houghton Mifflin, 1977.
Smith, Wendy. "PW Interviews Nicholas von Hoffman." *Publishers Weekly*, September 21, 1992, 72.
Von Hoffman, Nicholas. *Left at the Post*. Chicago: Quadrangle Books, 1970.

William Allen White
(1868–1944)

BORN ON FEBRUARY 10, 1868, to Mary Ann and Allen White in Emporia, Kansas, William Allen White was raised in El Dorado, Kansas, by parents who had different opinions. His mother, a teacher, was a Republican and his father, a doctor, was a Democrat. White leaned toward the Democrats when he was young, but he became a Republican when he realized that the Republicans represented change in Kansas.

White attended the Presbyterian College of Emporia, then the University of Kansas for several years; however, he left in 1890 without a degree. He worked as a reporter for the *El Dorado Republican*. In his spare time he wrote fiction and nonfiction.

White advocated against the Populists, who favored government regulation of railroads, a graduated income tax, and limited immigration, among other reforms. In short, he supported the Republicans. His writing was published in several publications, including the *Kansas City Journal*, which offered White a job in 1891. A year later, after an editor mishandled one of his stories, he quit. Within a few months he was working for the *Kansas City Star*, which was published by William Rockhill Nelson, whom White grew to respect primarily because Nelson believed strongly in exposing corruption.

In 1893, White married Sallie Lindsay, a teacher, and they started a family. He continued to work for the *Star*, but in 1895 purchased the *Emporia Gazette*, a small newspaper. Primarily as a result of his paper, White became an advocate for Emporia and Kansas, encouraging businesses to move to Emporia and Kansas. However, he became a national figure when he attacked William Jennings Bryan and the Populists in "What's the Matter with Kansas," which appeared in 1896. The editorial was published by other newspapers throughout the country. Later, it appeared in pamphlets. The same year his first collection of short stories, *The Real Issue: A Book of Kansas Stories*, was published.

White changed his mind about the Populists after meeting Theodore Roosevelt and reading his book *American Ideals* in 1897. Indeed, he became a strong supporter of Roosevelt and reform.

Two years later, *The Court of Boyville*, which contained stories that had appeared in *McClure's Magazine*, was published. This was followed by *Stratagems and Spoils: Stories of Love and Politics*, which was published in 1901.

In 1902, White continued to support Roosevelt in editorials and articles. Although his paper's circulation was only a couple of thousand, he contributed to the *Kansas City Star*, which reached a few hundred thousand readers. He also contributed material to the *Saturday Evening Post*, which reached thousands throughout the country.

White published *In Our Town*, another book of fiction, in 1906 and contributed advocacy articles to such magazines as the *Atlantic Monthly*, the *American Magazine*, for which he was an associate editor, and *Collier's*.

In 1908, he supported William Howard Taft for president, which pleased Roosevelt. However, when Taft became president, White changed his mind as a result of Taft's policies, including his firing of Richard Ballinger, the secretary of the interior, who had been accused of fraud. In 1909, he published *A Certain Rich Man*, a novel, which was followed in 1910 by *The Old Order Changeth: A View of American Democracy*, which was a collection of previously published articles about reforms.

In 1912, he supported Theodore Roosevelt for president, but Woodrow Wilson won. When World War I erupted in Europe in 1914, he paid attention to Germany's militarism. When the United

States entered the war in 1917, White supported the country in its efforts through the Committee on Public Information and through the Red Cross, which he wrote about in articles that were published in numerous papers across the country. His novel, *In the Heart of a Fool*, was published in 1918 and was criticized by critics. As a result, White stopped writing fiction.

White reported on the Versailles Peace Conference in 1919. The following year, he attended the Republican National Convention in Chicago, where Warren G. Harding won the nomination. Although Harding was not White's choice, he supported him.

Mary White, his teenage daughter, died while riding her horse in 1921. The day after her funeral he wrote a tribute to Mary, which was published in papers and read on radio programs.

White became a strong defender of the freedom of speech, including the press. He supported labor, including workers for railroads who had gone on strike. One of his editorials, "To an Anxious Friend," in which he defended free speech, won a Pulitzer Prize in 1923. White opposed the Ku Klux Klan, which influenced both political parties in Kansas. He ran for governor of Kansas in 1924, the year his biography, *Woodrow Wilson: The Man, His Times, and His Task*, was published. White lost the election.

In 1925, he published another biography, *Calvin Coolidge: The Man Who Is President*, about a politician he liked. Three years later he supported Herbert Hoover for president and attacked Hoover's opponent, Al Smith. To White, Hoover was progressive. However, as president, Hoover failed primarily because of the Great Depression, which gripped the country. In fact, most people blamed Hoover for it.

When Franklin D. Roosevelt sought reelection in 1936, White supported, with reservation, Alf Landon. When World War II erupted in Europe, White's son, William, served as a war correspondent. White headed the Committee to Defend America by Aiding the Allies, which attempted to persuade the public that military assistance to England would defeat Germany; as a result, the United States would not have to become directly involved.

White's health deteriorated in 1943; he died of a heart attack on January 29, 1944. His autobiography was published posthumously in 1946.

SELECTED WORKS

The Old Order Changeth: A View of American Democracy (1910)
The Editor and His People: Editorials by William Allen White (edited by Helen Ogden Mahin, 1924)
Forty Years on Main Street (compiled by Russell H. Fitzgibbon, 1937)
Speaking for the Consumer (1938)
Change Under Freedom (1939)
Objectives of the Committee to Defend America by Aiding the Allies (1940)

REFERENCES

Agran, Edward Gale. *Too Good a Town: William Allen White, Community, and the Emerging Rhetoric of Middle America.* Fayetteville: University of Arkansas Press, 1998.

Clough, Frank C. *William Allen White of Emporia.* New York: McGraw-Hill, 1941.

Griffith, Sally Foreman. *Home Town News: William Allen White and the Emporia Gazette.* New York: Oxford University Press, 1989.

Hinshaw, David. *A Man from Kansas: The Story of William Allen White.* New York: Putnam's, 1945.

Jernigan, E. Jay. *William Allen White.* Boston: Twayne, 1983.

Johnson, Walter. *William Allen White's America.* New York: Holt, 1947.

McKee, John DeWitt. *William Allen White: Maverick on Main Street.* Westport, Conn.: Greenwood, 1975.

Rich, Everett. *William Allen White: The Man from Emporia.* New York: Farrar & Rinehart, 1941.

White, William Allen. *The Autobiography of William Allen White.* New York: Macmillan, 1946.

Selected Bibliography

In addition to the references at the end of each entry, the following works may be helpful to readers who desire to learn more about advocacy journalism and its practitioners.

Backscheider, Paula R. *Daniel Defoe: His Life*. Baltimore: Johns Hopkins University Press, 1989.

Beasley, Maurine H., and Sheila Gibbons. *Taking Their Place: A Documentary History of Women and Journalism*. Lanham, Md.: University Press of America, 1993.

Belford, Barbara. *Brilliant Bylines: A Biographical Anthology of Notable Newspaperwomen in America*. New York: Columbia University Press, 1986.

Black, Jeremy. *The English Press in the Eighteenth Century*. Philadelphia: University of Pennsylvania Press, 1987.

Bleyer, Willard Grosvenor. *Main Currents in the History of American Journalism*. Boston: Houghton Mifflin, 1927.

Bond, Richmond P. *The Tatler: The Making of a Literary Journal*. Cambridge, Mass.: Harvard University Press, 1971.

Brendon, Piers. *The Life and Death of the Press Barons*. New York: Atheneum, 1983.

Bulman, David, ed. *Molders of Opinion*. Milwaukee, Wis.: Bruce, 1945.

Davidson, Philip. *Propaganda and the American Revolution, 1763–1783*. Chapel Hill: University of North Carolina Press, 1941.

Drewry, John E., ed. *Post Biographies of Famous Journalists*. Athens: University of Georgia Press, 1942.

Eisenstein, Elizabeth. *The Printing Press as an Agent of Change: Communications and Cultural Transformation in Early Modern Europe*. Cambridge: Cambridge University Press, 1979.

Fisher, Charles. *The Columnists*. New York: Howell, Soskin, 1944.

Ford, Edwin H., and Edwin Emery, eds. *Highlights in the History of the American Press: A Book of Readings*. Minneapolis: University of Minnesota Press, 1954.

Fowler, Gene. *Timber Line: A Story of Bonfils and Tammen*. New York: Covici, Friede, 1933.

Frank, Joseph. *The Beginnings of the English Newspaper: 1620–1660*. Cambridge, Mass.: Harvard University Press, 1961.

Hallin, Daniel C. *The "Uncensored War": The Media and Vietnam*. New York: Oxford University Press, 1986.

Hart, Jim Allee. *Views on the News: The Developing Editorial Syndrome, 1500–1800*. Carbondale: Southern Illinois University Press, 1970.

Heald, Morrell. *Transatlantic Vistas: American Journalists in Europe 1900–1940*. Kent, Ohio: Kent State University Press, 1988.

Hofstadter, Richard. *The Age of Reform: From Bryan to F.D.R.*. New York: Knopf, 1955.

Hosokawa, Bill. *Thunder in the Rockies: The Incredible "Denver Post."* New York: Morrow, 1976.

Hudson, Frederic. *Journalism in the United States, from 1690–1872*. New York: Harper, 1873.

Johnson, Icie F. *William Rockhill Nelson and the "Kansas City Star": Their Relation to the Development of the Beauty and Culture of Kansas City and the Middle West*. Kansas City: Burton, 1935.

Kessler, Lauren. *The Dissident Press: Alternative Journalism in American History*. Beverly Hills, Calif.: Sage, 1984.

Kobre, Sidney. *Development of American Journalism*. Dubuque, Iowa: Brown, 1969.

Kolko, Gabriel. *Confronting the Third World: United States Foreign Policy, 1945–1980*. New York: Pantheon Books, 1988.

Littlefield, Roy Everett. *William Randolph Hearst: His Role in American Progressivism*. Lanham, Md.: University Press of America, 1980.

Mahin, Helen O., ed. *The Editor and His People*. New York: Macmillan, 1924.

Marzolf, Marion. *Up from the Footnote: A History of Women Journalists*. New York: Hastings House, 1977.

McMurtrie, Douglas C., and Albert H. Allen. *Early Printing in Colorado: With a Bibliography of the Issues of the Press, 1859 to 1876, Inclusive, and a Record and Bibliography of Colorado Territorial Newspapers*. Denver: Hirschfeld, 1935.

Mock, James R., and Cedric Larson. *Words That Won the War: The Story of the Committee on Public Information, 1917–1919*. Princeton, N.J.: Princeton University Press, 1939.

Mott, Frank Luther. *American Journalism: A History, 1690–1960*. New York: Macmillan, 1962.

———. *A History of American Magazines*. 5 vols. Cambridge, Mass.: Harvard University Press, 1938–1968.

Mowry, George E. *Theodore Roosevelt and the Progressive Movement*. Madison: University of Wisconsin Press, 1946.

Murphy, James E., and Sharon M. Murphy. *Let My People Know: American Indian Journalism 1828–1978*. Norman: University of Oklahoma Press, 1981.

Nevins, Allan. *American Press Opinion, Washington to Coolidge: A Documentary Record of Editorial Leadership and Criticism, 1785–1927*. Boston: Heath, 1928.

Nye, Russel B. *Fettered Freedom: Civil Liberties and the Slavery Controversy, 1830–1860*. East Lansing: Michigan State University Press, 1963.

Painter, Nell Irvin. *Standing at Armageddon: The United States, 1877–1919*. New York: Norton, 1987.

Payne, George Henry. *History of Journalism in the United States*. New York: Appleton-Century-Crofts, 1920.

Perkin, Robert L. *The First Hundred Years: An Informal History of Denver and the "Rocky Mountain News."* Garden City, N.Y.: Doubleday, 1959.

Peterson, Theodore. *Magazines in the Twentieth Century*. Urbana: University of Illinois Press, 1964.

Pickett, Calder M. *Voices of the Past: Key Documents in the History of American Journalism*. Columbus, Ohio: Grid, 1977.

Schilpp, Madelon Golden, and Sharon M. Murphy. *Great Women of the Press*. Carbondale: Southern Illinois University Press, 1983.

Schlesinger, Arthur M. *Prelude to Independence: The Newspaper War on Britain, 1764–1776*. New York: Knopf, 1958.

Schneirov, Matthew. *The Dream of a New Social Order: Popular Magazines in America, 1893–1914*. New York: Columbia University Press, 1994.

Sorenson, Thomas C. *The Word War: The Story of American Propaganda*. New York: Harper & Row, 1968.

Stevens, John D. *Sensationalism and the New York Press*. New York: Columbia University Press, 1991.

Sullivan, Mark. *Our Times: the United States, 1900–1925*. 6 vols. New York: Scribner's, 1928–1935.

Tebbel, John, and Mary Ellen Zuckerman. *The Magazine in America: 1741–1990*. New York: Oxford University Press, 1991.

Thompson, John A. *Reformers and War: American Progressive Publicists and the First World War*. New York: Cambridge University Press, 1987.

Villard, Oswald Garrison. *Fighting Years: Memoirs of a Liberal Editor*. New York: Harcourt, Brace, 1939.

———. *Some Newspapers and Newspaper-men*. New York: Knopf, 1923.

Wood, James Playsted. *Magazines in the United States*. New York: Ronald, 1956.

Index

217

About the Author

Edd Applegate is professor in the School of Journalism, College of Mass Communication, at Middle Tennessee State University. He has written more than eighty chapters and entries for numerous books and encyclopedias, more than thirty articles for academic journals, and several scholarly books. He has also presented more than twenty articles at academic conferences.